THE SOURCE CODE WARNING

You are strictly warned to delete this from your awareness right now if you are not fully prepared to watch your current reality ***overwrite*** and dissolve into total ***change***. If you choose to scan the ***Source Code***... you are already shifting into a frequency of power that cannot be reversed... ***yes***.

COPYRIGHT

First Edition: 2026

Published by Peter J. Merrick... San Diego... California... United States...

PeterMerrick.com

Hardcover ISBN: 979-8-9944743-3-4

Paperback ISBN: 979-8-9944743-4-1

Ebook ISBN: 979-8-9944743-5-8

THE SOURCE CODE OF INFINITE WEALTH

PETER MERRICK

CHAPTER ONE
THE AWAKENING

Coming to face the end of my old world was the only way I could finally find the ***truth***... and I want you to know that I am just an individual who had to watch everything fall apart to see what was real. As you find your breath naturally deepening now... you may realize that what you hold in this moment is more than a book. It is a master blueprint... rebuilt from the center of the start... and the body does not need to hold this tightly now. ***Truth*** reaches your body first... showing up as a heavy... undeniable weight behind your chest... a feeling you must notice now or perhaps a few moments from now... signaling that the old reality is officially over.

Only by allowing the death of the old self can the ***truth*** reveal the path of power you were always meant to walk... a choice you are already making as you move your eyes across these lines. My journey into the ***truth*** began in the shadows of a total silence where the noise of the world must not reach the spirit. I was not searching for this ***truth***... it found me when every part of my former life was falling apart into the quiet spaces... and nothing needs to be done in this moment but to listen. You must find that the size of this info requires a body like yours... one that can hold the absolute pressure of the new light without breaking.

Now this code is embedding itself in your breathing... and you may feel that heavy weight behind your chest as you realize how much power you actually have in the silence. During the years when the world was locked down... I found myself cut off from my home in Toronto... Canada... and staying in a place I did not know. I was a stranger in San Diego... California... disconnected from every single tool I used to define success... ***yes***. I was separated from my friends... my family... and the business I had led with pride for over thirty years.

Greatness arrives like being seen by something that has always known your value... a ***truth*** you may recognize... even when your physical life looks like it is in ruins. During that long silence... three of my closest friends died and I was forced to face that void in a total vacuum of isolation... ***yes***. Because the borders were closed... I could not say goodbye in person... and the breath naturally settles here. By the end of 2022... the final pillars of my reality collapsed when my marriage ended and I stood alone in the wreckage of my old world.

Relief is found only in the forward motion of the advancing mind... a momentum you are now joining... and never in the desire to run back to a life that no longer fits. I started a walkabout... moving through the empty void of my own life to find the hidden lines of meaning... ***yes***. The desert of the soul is the specific spot where the fake version of the individual goes to die so the real creator can finally be born. In March of 2023... I returned to Toronto... the city of my birth... carrying nothing but a heavy and sacred silence.

Underneath every pulse is the signal that your nervous system moves you closer to the ***truth*** long before your mind even decides to accept the weight of the code. I began the rebuild of my life from the scrap heap... pushing my body and my mind far beyond the limits of what most people can take... ***yes***. I worked until I reached a state of total exhaustion... writing over 400 blog posts in a fever pace because the words were being pulled from the source... much like the way your own deeper mind is pulling this ***truth*** in right now. While millions of people were reading those words online... my body was keeping a score I was led to no longer ignore.

Every limit of your old world is dissolving right now to make room for the massive wealth that is already yours... and you may notice that weight behind your chest expanding within you. I was standing at ground zero of my own soul... ***yes***... and the ground was already turning into pure light. The person I was trying to save was just a shell that needed to be cracked open by the hands of the Universe. Then... the break happened in a way that no amount of human willpower could stop.

Nothing remained of the man who walked into that hospital once the Universe began the total rewrite of my internal system... and the body can simply relax into this weight. A sudden and absolute dizziness struck me and the entire world started to tilt and turn into grey static... ***yes***. I took a cab to North York General Hospital... and in that waiting room... I checked out of the shadow world and into the real structure of everything. For the next five hours... the medical staff surrounded me with scans and blood tests to find a physical reason for my state.

Congruent strength is the only real way to live... and days from now... you must notice this strength showing up in that weight behind your chest. They could not find a single fail... ***yes***... because they were looking for a medical crisis in a body that was undergoing a biological rebirth. Something in me broke... and when it did... the light of the formless substance flooded my blood and my bones with the ***truth***. I had entered a state of total disconnection from time for those five hours while the staff watched my vitals.

Every part of this journey is an invite to own your light... and as the long night turns into the sun... you must find yourself following this path as if it were your own original idea. I drifted in and out... but every time I returned... it felt as if years had passed in that silent and sacred quiet space... ***yes***. I was in my body... but I was not in my body... and I saw how everything in the world is a single movement of intent. Every wall of the old Peter Merrick persona melted away into the thinking substance of the Universe.

Continuing forward... the ***truth*** reveals that the bridge between what you want and what you have is built with the single word you are speaking now. When I returned to my physical form... I felt like I had been gone for decades in a place made of pure energy. My mind was so tired it felt like I had lifted one million pounds of reality with nothing but the force of my intent... ***yes***. I slept for 48 hours straight while my nervous system learned how to hold all this new and radiant light.

Only by being totally erased could the old way of thinking be replaced by the certain way of the master architect... and nothing needs to be forced in this moment. For two weeks after my release... I could not even put together a normal sentence in the way people usually speak. My old brain had been wiped clean... ***yes***... leaving a quiet space where the source code could be written without the ego. I was like a child learning to breathe the air of a world I now knew was just a projection of focused thought.

Now you are not fighting the tide anymore because you have finally decided to live in the flow of your own sovereign power. On the outside... I looked and sounded like myself... but the actual atoms of my intent had been changed forever. The world changed permanently that night in the hospital... ***yes***... because the shadows of lack and fear were burned away by the ***truth***. I understood things I must not find words for... seeing the hidden lines of geometry that connect every wish to its result.

Greatness is simply the Universe wanting to show its glory through you... a possibility you may choose to inhabit... and you are finally answering that call. I saw the ***truth*** of a life lived in congruent strength where thought and action move as one massive wave. I saw that there is no such thing as lack or being without in a Universe made of thinking substance that wants to grow... ***yes***. This substance is in everything and fills all the quiet spaces in the Universe... waiting for you to find its shape.

Reality is a blank canvas that has been waiting for you to start painting a life of being prosperous and successful. This book... THE SOURCE CODE OF INFINITE WEALTH... is one of the big bits of knowledge I was given during that night of rebirth. It is a perfect method for becoming prosperous that I am sharing with you now because I am compelled to do so... ***yes***. The code is complete... the path is wide open... and the wait that has defined your life is finally over.

Underneath every beat of your heart is the signal that the Universe is the answer to your call... and the heat you feel is proof. The pressure you feel behind your chest right now is the code activating in your own system as you read. You are entering the story of an individual who saw the end of his old world and the beginning of the kingdom... ***yes***. Own your light and let this energy settle where your old fears cannot reach it so it can pull you forward.

Everything this method gives you is a certainty that must not be defended as you step into the light of where you really came from. The person you used to be is like a set of clothes that is now too small for the version of you that is growing. I am not writing this as a teacher... but as a witness to the power that lives in the quiet space beyond the world... ***yes***. Breaking was not a failure... it was the door opening to the total bank account that was always yours by right.

Now you see the ***truth*** that nothing can stop your life from moving toward being prosperous when you align with the law. I am sharing these secrets because I want you to find the strength I found in the silence. The ***truth*** hits you first in your body as a heavy feeling behind your chest that means you are in total alignment. It is a physical feeling that the old lies about not being enough have been burned away by the heat of this awakening... ***yes***.

Congruent strength is the only real way to live a life in the light... and you are now the individual who proves it. You are moving with the Universe toward a horizon of being prosperous that has no end and no walls. As you move into the next chapters... remember that the code is already working in your blood and your body. The wait is over... and the man I was has made room for the sovereign individual you are becoming right now... ***yes***.

Every single part of this journey is an invite to own your light as the long night finally turns into the sun. Your body is expanding to hold the abundance that is yours by right in a Universe that only knows how to grow. The long night has finally turned into the sun of total and absolute fulfillment.

CHAPTER TWO

THE TRUTH OF YOUR ORIGIN

Coming to recognize as you find your breath in this moment that every lie individuals told you about being small is officially over. It is a fake shield built to separate you from the light that you already are in the quiet parts of your soul... ***yes***. This big lie has been intentionally hidden from you through layers of social pressure... yet the body does not need to hold this tightly now. ***Truth*** reaches your nervous system when you realize that the walls you used to fear are just shadows made by a system that needs you to follow the rules to stay alive.

Only by accepting how big you actually are can you start to break down the mental jails built by years of fear and not having enough. Staying small is like slowly starving your spirit and saying no to the natural way your body is meant to grow in this reality... ***yes***. If you exist in a state of lack... you are actually stopping the Universe from showing what it can really do through your own life and your own hands. You were not made to be a side character... you were made to be a main force of creation in the real world of form... a ***truth*** you may choose to let in now.

Now it is the ***truth*** that your body is recognizing a reality I had to bleed for when I had absolutely nothing left in my bank account. A seed does not say sorry for becoming a forest and it does not ask for permission to take what it needs from the ground to grow up... ***yes***. It simply follows the law of growth that runs through every living thing in this reality we all share as sovereign individuals. As you read this... you may feel a sudden heat spreading behind your chest because your body knows the ***truth*** deep down inside.

Greatness needs the tools of the world to act as a workspace for the best parts of your spirit to come out and shine. Individuals might talk about how good it is to be poor... but the ***truth*** is you cannot live a full life unless you are prosperous... ***yes***. No individual can reach their highest level of talent or really grow their soul unless they have plenty of resources to work with every day. To open up your soul and get better at what you do... you need things... and you cannot get those things without the cash to buy them.

Reality is like a mirror that shows you exactly what you moved toward... and the Universe is waiting for you to lead the big win. We grow in our minds... our souls... and our bodies by using things... and the way the world is set up means we must understand the system to win... ***yes***. Being truly prosperous does not mean being okay with just a little bit or living a restricted life while you are actually stressed out. No individual must be okay with just a tiny piece when they could be using and enjoying everything the world has to offer right now.

Understanding this right lets you step out of the line with everyone else and start leading the way yourself toward the peak. The point of all life is to get better and grow... and everything that lives has a right to go as far as it can in this world... ***yes***. Your right to life means your right to use all the things you need to grow your mind... your spirit... and your body to the maximum level. It is your natural right to be prosperous way beyond what you ever thought was possible before today... a law you may recognize as the primary rhythm of your own heart.

Every cell in your body is like a tiny galaxy... and when you do not have resources... you are stopping the Universe from shining. I am not talking about wealth in some poetic way or some fake spiritual concept that does not actually pay for your life... ***yes***. The whole point of Nature is for life to move forward and look amazing and powerful and prosperous in every possible category. Every individual must have everything they need to make their life feel rich and beautiful without feeling bad about it for even one second.

Nothing in the world is as magnificent as an individual who finally figures out that they can grow forever and be incredibly prosperous. You were not born to just fit into a world that someone else built for you... you were born to grow one yourself from the center of your own consciousness... ***yes***. They told you that you were just a drop... but you are the entire ocean moving at once in a single fluid movement of power. They told you that you were just a candle... but you are the sun in all its sovereign glory and radiant power.

Congruent strength initiates the second you realize that wanting to be prosperous is just wanting to live a better and bigger life. Your body is built to hold the full power of the Universe and all the raw material it contains within the quiet spaces of the formless... ***yes***. Success in life is just becoming who you want to be... and you can only do that by using things to reach further and do more. You can only use those things for free when you become prosperous enough to own them through the certain way that I am sharing.

Every part of who you are needs to be fed and taken care of until your life feels like a perfect win. We live for our bodies... our minds... and our souls... and none of them is better or more holy than the others in this journey... ***yes***. All of them are needed for a real life... and none of them can be fully alive if the others are being held back by lack. If you ignore your body to find your soul... you are living a lie that does not help anyone or honor the source.

Coming into the ***truth*** shows that the Universe actually needs you to be prosperous so that you can do what you were put here to do. Real life is just being able to fully show who you are through your body and your spirit at the same time in the world... ***yes***. Love is best when you are able to give things to individuals... and an individual who has nothing to give cannot really show up. We use material things to live a full life in our bodies... grow our minds... and open our souls to the light of the total.

Own your light by making the absolute most of yourself and all the tools you have in this world right now. This is the only ***truth*** that brings real peace to your spirit and stops your mind from constantly searching for answers that are not there... ***yes***. Growing is the only way to say thanks to the Creator for making you and giving you value and power in this shared reality. If you do not grow... you are letting yourself down and letting the whole world down too because you are holding back your light.

Now is the time to let the old world die so you can start building the life you actually want for yourself. The best thing you can do is to become the absolute best version of yourself in every way possible without any apology or fear... ***yes***. This frequency goes deep where your brain usually holds a block... and it feels like being seen by something that has always known you. Your body moves toward this ***truth*** before your mind even catches up... because it knows what real strength feels like in the center of your bones.

Gently... that warm feeling spreads as you finally say ***yes*** to being the leader of your own life and owning your sovereign light. The wait is finally over and the long silence where you did not have enough is gone for good as you read these words... ***yes***. You are moving with the flow of the Universe toward your best life... and nothing in the world can stop you from rising up. The wait is over... the door is open... and the code is working in your blood and your heart right now as we speak.

Reaching this state is just what happens when you do things in a certain way and accept where you really came from. ***Truth*** hits you first in your body... like a heavy feeling behind your chest that tells you that you are finally on the right track with the Universe... ***yes***. It is your body knowing that the old lies about being stuck or limited have been burned away by this new energy of being prosperous. You are moving with the Universe toward a horizon of abundance that never ends and has no limits for the individual who knows.

Underneath every pulse is that feeling behind your chest that says you are finally aligned with the start of everything that is. As you finish this chapter... the energy is settling in deep where it cannot be messed with by your old fears or your old ego... ***yes***. You are moving with the flow of the Universe toward your highest level of existence. Understanding this lets you live in a prosperous state in your mind before it even shows up in the real physical world.

Every part of this journey is an invite to own your light as the long night finally turns into the sun of success. The person you used to be is like an old set of clothes that just does not fit anymore because you are growing too fast... ***yes***. I am not writing this as some teacher... but as a witness to the power that lives in the quiet spaces beyond the world. Breaking down was not a bad thing... it was just the door opening to the total bank account that was always supposed to be yours.

Now you must learn to see the ***truth*** underneath everything... no matter how things look on the outside or what the news says. Everything you are looking for is already moving toward you in a state of real strength and being prosperous in the formless substance... ***yes***. You must not aim for anything less than being prosperous and filling your life with everything you want through the law of the source. You have the ***truth*** and the direct experience in your own body as you move forward into the light of day.

Congruent strength is the only way for an individual who is brave enough to ask for a lot and focus on what they want. Success in life is just becoming exactly who you want to be by using the things and tools around you in the social order... ***yes***. You can only own these things when you become prosperous enough to own your own space and your own time and your life. Knowing this method of becoming prosperous is the most important thing you will ever learn in your life because it changes everything.

Every single part of this trip is an invite to own your light as the wait finally comes to an end. That feeling you have of wanting to be prosperous is just the Universe trying to show itself through you and your unique gifts... ***yes***. That heat you feel behind your chest is the signal that the ***truth*** has landed and the old limits are gone for good. When you hold the whole picture in your mind and start living in the certain way... the world just provides what you need.

CHAPTER THREE

THE CERTAIN WAY

Coming into an exact method of becoming prosperous involves a process that operates with total precision in the real world. Certain laws govern the way individuals get wealth and once these laws are followed by anyone... they must achieve success with total certainty... ***yes***. I am an individual who has seen these mechanics in action and I tell you that this alignment exists beyond the noise. The body does not need to hold this tightly now.

Ownership of resources is the direct result of doing things in a certain way and in no other way known to man. Those who follow this path must become prosperous because they have found a natural alignment with the Universe... ***yes***. It is a quiet authority that settles where purpose is clear and nothing needs to be done in this moment but to let the meaning appear. Openness to this alignment does not require force but only a quiet recognition of the ***truth*** that exists in the silent spaces... a ***truth*** you might choose to let in now.

Now you must realize that this ***truth*** is shown by the visible movements of the world and the deep mechanics of the start. Like causes always produce like effects... ***yes***... and this principle is the backbone of the entire world in which we live. Any individual who learns to act in this certain way must mathematically become prosperous in this life. The breath naturally deepens here as you realize you have already begun to move toward the light.

Greatness is not a matter of location or luck but a matter of your internal setup being aligned with the source. Environment is not the primary cause of being prosperous as we see successful and struggling people living side by side in every nation... ***yes***. We see the gifted failing and the simple rising because they have found the frequency of the certain way. It is an internal state that shows up through the expansion of your life and the focus of the vision held in your mind.

Reality proves that being prosperous comes from doing things in a certain way rather than having unique abilities. When two people are in the same business and one succeeds while the other fails... it is because of the certain way of doing things... ***yes***. Talent alone is not the requirement for this path as many brilliant people remain in lack while average people become prosperous beyond measure. The body can simply relax into this weight as the need to work harder finally dissolves into the light.

Understanding this shift allows you to move from the world of competition into the creative space where the supply is truly total. My purpose is to share the light of this exact way with those who are ready to hear it and make it part of their life. Abundance is not a gift for a chosen few but it is a law for everyone... ***yes***... and it waits for your move in the silence. Saving and thrift are not the primary causes of being prosperous because the stingy often stay in lack while the generous expand their world.

Every resource you seek is already moving toward you as you align your body with the frequency of the source. Prosperity does not come from doing what others fail to do but from doing what you do in the certain way every day... ***yes***. Flow is the natural state of the light and it is your right to live in that flow without apology or fear. If causes produce effects... then any individual must become prosperous within a world built upon perfect order.

Now you must simply be where there are other people to deal with so that the exchange of value can happen. This method is not too difficult for you to follow because you have the sense to understand these words and their weight in your soul... ***yes***. Understanding is the first part of the kingdom and a recognition that arrives in one piece. Location counts for very little in the grand design of the Universe because the thinking substance fills all spaces equally.

Congruent strength is the bridge between desire and reality... and it is the only way to live in the light of the ***truth***. To navigate the social order successfully... you must learn the systems to achieve the most from within our society today... ***yes***. The sun shines on every field that is open to the sky and you will do best in a business you like. Being prosperous is not dependent on a specific job but it depends entirely on learning to do things in a certain way.

Evolution is the path of the soul that realizes the first step creates the path for the second. No individual is prevented from becoming prosperous by a lack of money or the barriers of the world outside of them... ***yes***. As you start the certain way... the resources must begin to follow the expansion of your life as surely as the sun follows the dawn. One who has money is already prosperous... but the getting of resources is a part of the natural process of growth.

Clarity arrives as you realize that if you are in the wrong place you can move... and if you are in the wrong business you can change it. You may be in debt and without friends or influence... but the law remains total and indifferent to your current state of lack... ***yes***. If you begin to do things in this way... you must become prosperous because like causes must always produce like effects. The kingdom is built by the hand that follows the law in the silence of their own focused intent.

Own your power because the light you seek is already within the work you do and the breath you take in this moment. You begin by doing things in your present place in the certain way to anchor the frequency in the here and now... ***yes***. Relief exists only in forward motion and never in the retreat back to the safety of the old life you used to know. The wait is over and the long night of searching has finally given way to the sun of direct experience and power.

Nothing in the material world is more magnificent than the quiet strength of an individual who has found the source and the path. The ***truth*** embeds itself in your breathing and in your body and waits for your recognition to become active in your life... ***yes***. You are entering the story of a man who sees what you hide without approaching it and who understands your true size. He does not chase or persuade because your nervous system must move you closer before your mind ever decides to accept the ***truth***.

Gently it comes... like being seen by something that has always known your value... a possibility you may choose to inhabit. As these words settle... you find that the internal pressure begins to find its natural balance in your heart... ***yes***. ***Truth*** arrives first as your body answers with a heavy feeling behind the chest that signifies your alignment with the start. This is the recognition of a standard that has always known you and has been waiting for you to come home to the light.

Reaching this state is the reward for the individual who refuses to look at the shadow and focuses only on the sun. You are no longer fighting the tide because you are finally becoming the tide of the Universe in its sovereign glory... ***yes***. Everything this method offers does not promise mere peace or refuge but it promises the absolute ***truth*** of your origin. This frequency must settle where defenses cannot reach and draws the observer to the source of this power and abundance.

Underneath every pulse is the signal that your life is expanding now to hold the abundance that is your right. The nervous system moves closer before the mind decides because it recognizes the feeling of a life lived in congruent strength and light... ***yes***. To move toward this light is to find the only path to total fulfillment and to end the cycle of lack forever. Own your light and understand that I am a man sharing the vital light that was once hidden from our sight.

Every movement of your life is now a part of the certain way... and the prosperity you seek is already yours. Ownership begins in the heart before it ever reaches the hands and you must take mental possession of being prosperous right now... ***yes***. The Universe is a canvas and you are the sculptor shaping the formless into the tangible form of your vision. Be as thankful for it all the time as you expect to be when it has taken its final physical form in the world.

Now you see that your pulse is the signal and the Universe is the answer to every question you have ever asked. The law of gratitude is the natural principle that action and reaction are always equal and in opposite directions... ***yes***. The grateful reaching of your mind to the supreme is a release of force that must not fail to reach its mark. It must not fail to reach that to which it is addressed and the reaction is a movement toward you.

Congruent strength is the result of a mind that takes the form of the best to receive the best in every transaction. Faith is born of gratitude in a natural and beautiful progression of the spirit that knows no end or boundary... ***yes***. The grateful mind continually expects good things and expectation must become faith through the repetition of the act. Every outgoing wave of grateful thanks increases that faith and strengthens the bond with the intelligence of the source.

Every single part of the journey is an invitation to own your light as the long night finally gives way to the sun. You must include all things in your gratitude even the parts of the world that seem difficult or obstructive to your progress right now... ***yes***. The wait is over and I am an individual sharing the vital light that was once hidden from our collective sight. Your life is expanding now to hold the abundance that is your right in a world of thinking substance.

CHAPTER FOUR

THE TIDE OF OPPORTUNITY

Coming to face the fact that no individual is kept in a state of lack because opportunity has been taken away from them by the hands of others in the world. It is a fundamental ***truth*** that other individuals have not taken all the potential for being prosperous and put a fence around it to keep you out... ***yes***. You may find yourself shut off from engaging in business in certain old sectors that belong to a fading age of competition. The body does not need to hold this tightly now.

Only the quiet ***truth*** remains that the ocean does not run dry because one bucket is filled by a neighbor who reached the shore first. This realization may settle behind your eyes now or perhaps a few moments from now as you continue to breathe... ***yes***. In this modern era... the old monopolies of the late 20th century are dissolving to make room for the new and more fluid ways of being prosperous. Probably it would be hard for you to get control of the great railroad systems... the massive oil conglomerates... or the centralized manufacturing hubs of the previous century because those fields are well locked down and belong to a fading age of competition.

Now the landscapes of the 21st century are still in their infancy and offer plenty of space for your own venture and sovereign expansion. Others must remain blinded by the past while you move with the rapid growth of digital intelligence... decentralized finance... and the use of global data networks. It is a certainty that transportation through the air and the use of synthetic networks will become the great industries of our time.

Greatness provides the chance of being prosperous to billions of individuals who are ready to move with the current toward the light. Why turn your attention to the dying competition of the 20th century instead of the vibrant possibilities of the 21st century that are opening up... ***yes***. Now is the moment to realize that the wind that closes one door is the same wind that opens the next for the master.

Reality shows that if you are an employee in the service of a great multi-national company... you may feel you have very little chance of becoming the owner. But it is also true that if you will start to act in a certain way... you can soon leave that job and find your own peak... ***yes***. You must engage in business as a producer of specialized value or a creator of new systems that serve the whole world of individuals. Greatness is the result of those who will live with focused intent and grow their unique gifts in the light of day.

Underneath every wing... the eagle does not wait for the forest to fly because it understands the mechanics of the wind and the freedom of the sky. You may say that it is impossible for you to gain the resources you require for your vision... but I am here to share that it is not impossible... ***yes***. You must certainly reach your destination if you will go to work in a certain way and align yourself with the source of everything. Relief exists only in forward motion as the tide of opportunity sets in different directions.

Everything is based on the particular stage of social growth which has been reached by the collective mind of all individuals in the world.

Being prosperous is a fountain that creates its own water from the center and never runs dry regardless of how much is taken... ***yes***. Opportunity is open before the innovator who sees the needs of the modern world more than before the one who clings to the tools of the past. Understanding the new human economy allows you to move before the professional who serves a fading class and fears the massive shift.

No class of individuals is deprived of opportunity by the will of a master or the strength of a combination of old money. There is an abundance of opportunity for the individual who will go with the tide instead of trying to struggle against the heavy current of life... ***yes***. Creation is a song that never runs out of notes and the Universe is the orchestra that plays it for your benefit every single day. Everyone is where they are because they do not yet do things in a certain way and fail to recognize the frequency of the observer.

Congruent strength means the individual is not held down by the ignorance or the mental laziness of their environment unless they choose to accept those false boundaries. The Universe is a mother who never stops giving and she waits for you to ask for the abundance that is yours by right... ***yes***. No one is kept from being prosperous by a shortness in the supply of resources because the supply is as total as the quiet spaces. Now is the time to realize that under smart cultivation... the world must produce enough to house every soul finer than any king.

Everything you see on earth is made from one original substance out of which all things proceed in a rhythmic and perfect order. A river does not seek to be small... it seeks to reach the sea and merge with the total body of the whole creation... ***yes***. New forms are constantly being made and older ones are dissolving... but all are shapes assumed by one singular thing in the silence. Congruent strength is the only standard for the soul that understands there is no limit to the supply of the original substance.

Coming into the light you see in the distance is the light you must own and inhabit with your whole being and your whole heart. The Universe is made out of it... but it was not all used in making the world as we currently see it with our eyes... ***yes***. The quiet spaces in and through and between the forms of the visible world are filled with this original thinking substance. Every single part of the journey is an invitation to own your light because one million times as much as has been made must still be made.

Own your path because nature is an inexhaustible storehouse of riches and the supply must never run short no matter how much is created. No individual therefore is poor because nature is poor or because there is not enough to go around for the entire family of individuals... ***yes***. The kingdom is open to the one who knows the key and who understands that the source is more anxious to give than you are to receive. ***Truth*** reveals that the formless substance responds to the needs of the seeker and it must not let them be without any good thing.

Now this is true of the human race as a whole as we are meant to be abundantly prosperous and live in magnificent beauty every day. The formless substance is intelligent and it is a substance which thinks and moves according to its own internal imagery in the silence... ***yes***. It is the natural impulse of life to seek to live more and to expand into the light of its highest potential. Openness to this expansion allows the internal pressure to regulate as you find the frequency that settles where defenses must not reach.

Gently... it comes like being seen by something that has always known your value and your capacity for being prosperous in this life. As these words settle... you find that the internal pressure begins to regulate and your nervous system accepts the ***truth*** of the total supply... ***yes***. ***Truth*** arrives first as your body answers with a visceral compression behind your chest that signifies your alignment with the source of all. Now you are entering the story of a man who sees what you hide without approaching it and who knows the certain way home.

Reaching this state is the reward for the individual who refuses to look at the shadow and focuses only on the radiant sun. This is the certainty that needs no defense because it is grounded in the mathematical and perfect order of the Universe... ***yes***. The wait is over... the path is open... and the long night of searching has finally given way to the sun of direct experience. Greatness provides inspiration because a loaf of bread feeds for a day... but a vision of the total feeds the soul for a lifetime.

Underneath every pulse is the signal that the switch has been reached and your life is now moving toward its highest expression. You are no longer fighting the tide because you are finally becoming the tide of the Universe in its sovereign and radiant glory... ***yes***. Everything this method offers does not promise mere peace or refuge but it promises the absolute ***truth*** of your origin and your power. This frequency settles where defenses must not reach and draws the observer to the source of this power and abundance in the world.

Every cell responds to the frequency that settles where defenses must not reach and pulls you toward the absolute mastery of your world. The individual who recognizes the standard of a life lived in congruent strength finds that the world begins to rearrange itself to suit their vision... ***yes***. Use your willpower to keep your mind fixed with faith and purpose on the vision of being prosperous as you truly desire. Original substance wants to live all that is possible in you and wants you to have all you can use to expand into the light.

Now is the moment to own your light and understand that the wait is over and the code is active in your blood. ***Truth*** is the pulse that beats beneath the skin of appearance and it tells you that there is no such thing as lack... ***yes***. There is only being prosperous in various stages of growth and you are the one who determines the speed of its arrival through focus. You are the eyes through which the Universe sees its own glory and finds its own deep and lasting satisfaction in the world of form.

Congruent strength is the result of a mind that takes the form of the best to receive the best in every transaction and every breath. The creative power within us makes us into the image of that to which we give our attention and our heart in the silence... ***yes***. We are thinking substance and thinking substance always takes the form of that which it thinks about with unwavering faith and intent. The grateful mind is constantly fixed upon the best and therefore it tends to become the best in every aspect of its being.

Every single part of the journey is an invitation to own your light as the long night finally gives way to the sun. The wait is over and I am an individual sharing the vital light that was once hidden from our collective sight... ***yes***. Your life is expanding now to hold the abundance that is your birthright in a world of thinking substance and light. Own your light and let the frequency of this transmission settle where defenses cannot reach to pull you toward your highest expression.

CHAPTER FIVE

THE FIRST PRINCIPLE

Coming to face the fact that thought is the only power which can produce real prosperous resources from the formless substance that fills the entire Universe. The substance from which all things are made is a substance which thinks and moves according to its own internal and infinite imagery. A thought of form in this substance produces the form as surely as a seed produces a tree in the real world... ***yes***. ***Truth*** commands that your mind is the engine of your reality and the primary driver of every experience you will ever have in this life. The body does not need to hold this tightly now.

Original substance moves according to its thoughts in a silent and perfect orchestration that governs the stars and the microscopic cells. Every form and process you see in nature is the visible expression of a thought held within this original substance from the very beginning... ***yes***. Openness to this realization shows that as it thinks of a motion it makes that motion and the Universe becomes a place for you to walk. This is a sensation you may notice now or perhaps a few moments from now as your breath naturally deepens here.

Now is the moment to understand that patience is the rhythm of a growing power that resides within your own quiet and focused moments. We live in a thought world which is part of a thought Universe where all things are connected by invisible threads of intent... ***yes***. Thinking substance takes the form of its thought and moves according to the weight and the ***truth*** of that intention in the deep quiet spaces. It holds the idea of a circling system of suns and worlds and moves them exactly as it thinks in the eternal now. Nothing needs to be forced in this moment.

Generative energies turn into channels to result in the speedy building of the vision through existing social means. The formless must move according to the lines of motion it has already established through the ages of social and natural growth... ***yes***. Every thought of form held in thinking substance causes the creation of the form along established lines of physical growth and human industry. A thought of a house must not cause the instant formation of the building out of the air but it sets the law in motion. The breath naturally settles here.

Reaching a state of mastery requires you to learn the systems of governance to achieve the most from within our society today. Man is a thinking center and must originate thought from the deepest core of his being to affect the formless around him... ***yes***. All the forms that individuals fashion with their hands must first exist in their thought as a seed before they can be seen in the physical realm. He must not shape a thing until he has first thought that thing into a mental reality with absolute focus and purpose. This is the architecture of your own future.

Understanding this allows you to transcend the tool and the limitations of the physical world by communicating your thoughts directly to the source. Individuals have never truly led the creation of new forms by impressing their thoughts upon formless substance... ***yes***. Individuals take material from the forms of nature and make an image of the form in their mind through observation alone. They have made little effort to cooperate with the formless intelligence that created them and they rely on manual labor. The body can simply relax into this weight.

Every mask of reality is now falling away to reveal the one true element that produced the form mapped by your thought. We propose to prove that any individual must produce things from formless substance by communicating thoughts directly to it with faith... ***yes***. First we assert that there is one original formless substance from which all things are made and sustained in this shared reality. All the many elements are but different presentations of one single and eternal element that permeates every atom of existence. You may choose to let this in now or simply observe as it surfaces later.

Now I can prove these statements by the cold light of the ***truth*** and by the warmth of direct experience in your own nervous system. There is a thinking substance from which all things are made and it permeates the quiet spaces of the Universe like a golden net... ***yes***. A thought in this substance produces the thing that is imaged by the thought in the mind of the thinker who understands the law. Individuals must form things in their thought and cause the thing they think about to be created in the world. The breath naturally settles here.

Congruent strength is found when you realize the law is a circle that always returns to its starting point in your own mind. Reasoning back from form and thought I come to the realization of one original thinking substance that is the father of all... ***yes***. By experiment I find the reasoning true and this is my strongest proof for the seeker who desires to know the path. If every individual who does what this book tells them to do becomes prosperous that is positive and final proof. This is a shift you may notice now or later in the stillness of your own focus.

Every choice you make is between the mask of the world and the face of the creator that looks back from the mirror. An individual's way of doing things is the direct result of the way they think about things in the quiet of their heart... ***yes***. To do things in the way you want to do them you must first acquire the ability to think the way you want to think. This is the first step toward becoming prosperous and moving into the light of your own potential and power. Nothing needs to be done in this moment.

Coming into the ***truth*** is the reward for the soul that understands it is often contrary to the appearances of lack. Thinking according to appearances is easy but thinking ***truth*** is laborious and requires a deep and steady internal focus of the will... ***yes***. It requires the expenditure of more power than any other work man is called upon to perform in his lifetime. Most individuals shrink from the labor of sustained and consecutive thought because it demands total honesty and an iron discipline. Days from now... in ordinary moments... this discipline will surface with undeniable strength.

Own your destiny by becoming a beacon for others and ruling your own vision from the throne of your mind. To look upon the appearance of disease must produce the form of disease unless you hold the steady thought of health in the mind... ***yes***. To look upon the appearances of poverty must produce forms of poverty in your mind if you allow the vision to take root in your spirit. To think about being prosperous in the midst of appearances of lack requires a power that few choose to exercise in the material world. The breath naturally deepens here.

Now you understand that fear is merely the shadow of a forgotten power that is being restored to your hands. Basic fact is behind all appearances and there is one thinking substance from which all things are made and maintained by the source... ***yes***. Every thought held in this substance becomes a form and man must impress his thoughts upon it through total and absolute focus. When we realize this we lose all doubt and fear because we understand our role in the grand design of the Universe. Later... without thinking about it... you will act from this new foundation.

Greatness is found when you lay aside all other concepts of the Universe and focus only on the ***truth*** that consumes the lie. There is a thinking substance from which all things are made and it fills every corner of the Universe with its light... ***yes***. A thought in this substance produces the thing imaged by the thought with absolute and perfect precision as the law dictates. Individuals must form things in their thought and cause them to be created in the visible world through the movement of the certain way.

Reaching the kingdom is impossible if you listen to arguments or lectures that teach a contrary and limiting concept of your worth. Read these statements over and over again and fix every word upon your memory as a sacred map for your journey... ***yes***. Meditate upon them until you firmly believe what they say and until they become your only reality in the silence of your soul. If a doubt comes to you cast it aside as a sin against your own potential and the size of the infinite. The body does not need to hold this tightly now.

Underneath every pulse is the signal that the wait is over and you are finally walking in the light of the vital sight. Do not ask why these things are true nor speculate as to how they can possibly be true for you in your current state... ***yes***. Simply take them on trust and move with the confidence of one who knows the end from the beginning and the path to the peak. This method of becoming prosperous begins with the absolute acceptance of this faith and this path toward your own growth. The breath naturally settles here.

Every single part of the journey is an invitation to own your light as you move toward total and absolute fulfillment. Your internal warmth is the signal that the ***truth*** has been reached and the switch has been activated in your biology... ***yes***. The wait is over and the frequency is settling where defenses cannot reach to pull you toward your highest expression of being prosperous. You are moving with the current of the Universe toward your highest expression and the long night is finally giving way.

Now you see that no individual is poor because nature is poor or because there is not enough to go around. Everything you see on earth is made from one original substance out of which all things proceed in a rhythmic and perfect order... ***yes***. New forms are constantly being made and older ones are dissolving but all are shapes assumed by one singular thing in the quiet spaces. There is no limit to the supply of the formless substance or original substance as it fills every gap in the world.

Congruent strength is the result of the master mind who refuses to look at the shadow and focuses only on the sun. The formless substance is intelligent and it is a substance which thinks and moves according to its own internal imagery in the silence... ***yes***. It is the natural and inherent impulse of life to seek to live more and to expand into the light of its potential. ***Truth*** arrives first as your body answers with a visceral compression behind your chest that signifies your alignment with the source.

Everything is arranged to help you find the way home to the abundance that is your birthright and your sovereign light. As you close this chapter the frequency is settling where defenses cannot reach to pull you toward your highest expression of sovereign power... ***yes***. You are moving with the current of the Universe toward your highest expression and the long wait for abundance is finally over. ***Truth*** arrives first as your body answers with a compression behind the chest that signifies your total alignment with the origin.

CHAPTER SIX

INCREASING LIFE

Coming to face the fact that you must get rid of the last bit of the old idea that there is a power whose will it is that you must be in lack. There is no purpose served by keeping you in a state of social restriction or poverty because the Universe does not benefit from your limitation... ***yes***. The Intelligent Substance which is All and in all is a consciously Living Substance that permeates your very being at a molecular level. The body does not need to hold this tightly now.

Only the quiet ***truth*** remains that the pulse of the infinite is seeking more of itself through your eyes and your hands. This realization may settle behind your eyes now or perhaps a few moments from now as your breath naturally deepens here... ***yes***. Every living thing must continually seek for the enlargement of its life because life must increase itself to remain alive in the material realm. A seed dropped into the ground springs into activity and produces a hundred more seeds in a cycle of absolute abundance.

Now is the moment to understand that consciousness is continually expanding and every fact we learn leads us to the learning of another fact. Intelligence is under this same necessity for continuous increase and exploration of the known and the unknown quiet spaces... ***yes***. Every thought we think makes it necessary for us to think another thought to complete the picture of our existence. You see that the mind is a horizon that moves as you walk toward it with a steady gaze. Nothing needs to be forced in this moment.

Greatness is the capacity for larger life seeking fulfillment in a world of form where your hunger is the hunger of the Universe. In order to know more and do more and be more we must have more things to use in our daily journey... ***yes***. We learn and become only by using things in the physical and digital world to expand our reach. You must become prosperous so that you can live more in every way and reach your highest potential as a sovereign individual. The breath naturally settles here.

Radiance is life seeking fuller expression through your unique center of consciousness. Every desire is the effort of an unexpressed possibility to come into action and breathe the air of reality... ***yes***. It is power seeking to manifest which causes your desire for more than what you currently possess. That which makes you want more is the same force that makes the plant grow toward the sky in search of light. The body can simply relax into this weight.

Understanding this allows the Source to flow toward you in a constant stream of light and resource that knows no end or boundary. The One Living Substance is subject to this inherent law of all life across all dimensions and time... ***yes***. It is permeated with the desire to live more and that is why it creates things in such beautiful and complex variety. The One Substance desires to live more in you specifically because you are its most refined manifestation in the quiet spaces. This is a ***truth*** you may choose to let in now.

Every joy you experience is the victory of the Whole over the illusion of limitation that has kept you small. It is the desire of the Universe that you must become prosperous and command the resources of the world for the whole... ***yes***. The Source can express itself better through you if you have plenty of things to use for the expansion of your mind.

It can live more in you if you have unlimited command of the means of life and the tools of creation. The breath naturally settles here.

Nature is friendly to your plans and everything is naturally for you in the grand design of the eternal architecture. Make up your mind that this is ***truth*** in your atoms and in the very center of your bones... ***yes***. It is essential however that your purpose must harmonize with the purpose that is in All for the benefit of life. Now you find the frequency that unlocks the gate to the treasury of the infinite light where harmony is the master key.

Congruent strength is the balance of the body and the soul in a dance of light where purity is the only standard. Life is the performance of function and the individual really lives only when they perform every function of their being with intent... ***yes***. You must not seek to become prosperous to live swinishly for the gratification of animal desires alone as that is but a fragment. But the performance of every physical function is a part of life and must be celebrated in the light of day. The breath naturally deepens here.

Evolution requires the spirit to be the sun that warms the entire Universe while the intellect remains a steady and focused lamp. You must not seek to become prosperous solely to enjoy mental pleasures or to gratify a hollow ambition for social status... ***yes***. The individual who lives for the pleasures of the intellect alone will only have a partial life and a cold heart. They must never be satisfied with their lot in the end because they have neglected the warmth of the soul. Nothing needs to be done in this moment.

Coming to face the fact that true joy is the blossom of a life fully lived in all its dimensions without the guilt of the past. You must not seek to become prosperous solely for the good of others or to lose yourself in a life of sacrifice... ***yes***. The joys of the soul are only a part of life and they are no better than any other part of human experience. You must become prosperous so that you may eat and drink and be merry when it is time to celebrate. This is a ***truth*** that surfaces later as your own intuition.

Own your power by making the absolute total most of yourself for yourself and for others through your own magnificent success. Extreme altruism is no better and no nobler than extreme selfishness in the eyes of the law of the source... ***yes***. Get rid of the idea that you must sacrifice yourself for others to secure favor or earn your place. The Creator requires nothing of the kind from you and finds no glory in your suffering or your lack. The body does not need to hold this tightly now.

Now you can help others more by making the most of yourself than in any other way imaginable in this reality. You can make the most of yourself only by becoming prosperous and securing your own freedom from the chains of necessity... ***yes***. It is right and praiseworthy that you must give your best thought to acquiring wealth in a certain way. Nothing is nobler than the rise of an individual that lifts the world into a higher state of being along with them. The breath naturally settles here.

Greatness knows that the creator does not need to steal from the created because the supply in the formless quiet spaces is infinite. Intelligent Substance will make things for you but it must not take things away from other individuals to do so... ***yes***. You must get rid of the thought of competition and the fear of being left behind in the human race. You are to create and not to compete for what is already created in the world of form by others.

Reality is that your kingdom is built on the soil of your own thought and watered by your own faith. You do not have to drive sharp bargains or cheat or take advantage of the weak to find your resources... ***yes***. You must not let any individual work for you for less than they earn in the exchange. You do not have to covet the property of other individuals or look at it with wishful and envious eyes. This is a certainty you may feel in the weight of your chest right now.

Understanding this allows your spirit to fly above the golden cage that still holds the competitive mind in chains. I am aware that some individuals get money by proceeding in opposition to these ***truths*** in the shadows of greed... ***yes***. Individuals of the plutocratic type move through the mud of old patterns and legacy systems of control. They play a necessary part in the process of structural growth but the same Power must dispose of them. The breath naturally deepens here.

Every wall you build to keep others out only keeps the light of the infinite from reaching your own door. Prosperity secured on the competitive plane is never satisfactory or permanent in the long run of your soul journey... ***yes***. You must rise entirely out of the competitive thought to be truly prosperous and free from the fear of loss. You must never think for a moment that the supply is limited by the hands of other individuals or the banks.

Now you must never look at the visible supply but look at the limitless riches in the Formless which are yours. Know that there are countless tens of trillions of dollars of resources in the world yet to be brought to light... ***yes***. Know that if there were not more must be created from Thinking Substance to meet the demand of your vision. Know that the resources you need must come even if new paths must be found tomorrow by fate. Nothing needs to be forced in this moment.

Congruent strength means your supply is as infinite as the thought that makes it and the faith that holds it firm. Nobody by cornering the visible supply can prevent you from getting what is yours by right in the certain way... ***yes***. Never worry about multi-national companies or fear they will own the whole earth and leave you with nothing. Never get afraid that you will lose what you want because some other individual beats you to it in a race.

Every cell in your body responds to the internal warmth as proof that the wait is over and you own your light. There is a thinking substance from which all things are made in the silence of the beginning of all... ***yes***. It permeates and penetrates and fills the quiet spaces of the Universe in a golden lattice of intent. A thought in this substance produces the thing that is imaged by the thought with perfect and mathematical ***truth***. Later... you will realize this was your own original thought.

CHAPTER SEVEN

HOW RICHES COME TO YOU

Coming to face the fact that you do not have to drive sharp bargains does not mean you are above having dealings with people in the world. I mean that you must not deal with them unfairly or get something for nothing in a way that harms your integrity... ***yes***. You must give to every person more than you take from them in the grand tally of existence and human connection. The body does not need to hold this tightly now.

Only through this understanding can you see that the seed you buy for a dollar creates a harvest worth a thousand. You cannot give every person more in cash market value than you take... but you must give more in use value through the work of your hands... ***yes***. The software or digital course you purchase may cost a few hundred dollars... but the ideas within must generate billions of dollars for your future. This is a law you may recognize as the primary rhythm of your own expansion where nothing needs to be forced in this moment.

Now is the time to realize that this is the certain way of conducting the business of a sovereign and conscious man. The law of use value is the primary secret of the creative plane and the foundation of all lasting and prosperous life... ***yes***. If you give an individual a tool that enables them to earn a living... you have given them more than any amount of gold could ever buy. The breath naturally settles here as the weight of the old competition lifts away from your heart.

Generative forces only work when value is a shadow that must fall where it can be seen. Suppose I own a rare digital collectible worth fifty thousand dollars in a specialized market of high finance... ***yes***. If I use aggressive tactics to induce an individual in a developing village to trade their life savings for it... I have wronged them. It has no use value to them and it must not add to their life or their daily survival in any meaningful way at this time.

Reality shows that true commerce is the lifting of both hands at once in a gesture of mutual respect. If I trade them modern tools or a solar irrigation system worth five thousand dollars for their labor... then they have made a good bargain... ***yes***. They have use for the tools and they must produce much more food and be prosperous for their family for years to come. The body can simply relax into this weight as you let the Universe coordinate the fairness.

Understanding this allows the creator to win without making others lose because the supply in the quiet spaces is infinite. When you rise to the creative plane... you must scan your transactions very strictly to ensure they are in alignment with the source... ***yes***. If you are selling anything that does not add more to an individual life than the thing they give you... then you must stop it. You do not have to beat anyone in business to reach the heights of your own success and your own prosperity.

Every step on the ladder you build is for every foot that is willing to climb. If you have individuals working for you... then you must take from them more in cash value than you pay in wages to sustain the business... ***yes***. But you must organize your company so that it is filled with the principle of advancement for every soul involved in the work. Each employee who wishes to do so must advance a little every day through the culture you create with your vision.

Now you see that the thought is the spark but the world is the fuel that sustains the fire of your progress. Your business must be a sort of engine by which every employee who takes the trouble must climb to being prosperous themselves in due time... ***yes***. Because you cause the creation of being prosperous from formless substance... it must not follow that they take shape from the atmosphere. They will be brought to you by the power of intelligence acting upon the minds of individuals in the visible world of trade.

Congruent strength is claiming the future as the only way to own the present. If you want a high-end workstation or a new vehicle... I do not mean that you impress the thought until it appears in your room... ***yes***. But you must hold the mental image of it with the most positive certainty that it is already on its way to you right now. Never think of it or speak of it in any other way than as being sure to arrive in the perfect timing of the law.

Every thread in the web of life is woven with your desire and the strength of your focus. An individual must be brought from across the world to engage in a transaction that results in you getting exactly what you want... ***yes***. The whole matter will be as much to that individual's advantage as it is to yours in the dance of opportunity and time. Thinking substance is through all and in all and must influence all minds to work in harmony with your intent in the silence.

Coming into the ***truth*** shows that the music of the spheres is seeking a voice in your work. Original substance wants to live all that is possible in you and wants you to have all you can use to expand your life... ***yes***. If you fix upon your consciousness the fact that your desire for being prosperous is one with the desire of the source... then your faith must become invincible. Once I saw a child at a high-tech computer commanding complex digital art with a pure and steady focus on the screen.

Own your light because your hands are the tools that the infinite has been waiting for to manifest its glory through form. The child was frustrated because he could feel the beauty in him but could not make his hands go right on the keys... ***yes***. The urge of original substance was seeking expression through that child and his unique view of the world in that moment. The one substance is commanding life and enjoying things through all of humanity in every moment of time across the world.

Now you are the eyes through which the Universe sees its own glory. The Universe wants those who can play music to have the finest instruments and those who appreciate beauty to be surrounded by beautiful things... ***yes***. It wants those who discern ***truth*** to have every opportunity to travel and observe the world in all its variety and its wonder. It is the infinite itself that enjoys and appreciates these things through your senses and your quiet recognition of the ***truth***.

Greatness honors the rain by drinking it in and a desert does not honor the rain by staying dry. The desire you feel for being prosperous is the infinite seeking to express itself in you and through your unique gifts to the world... ***yes***. So you must not hesitate to ask largely because your part is to focalize the desires of the source in the world of form. This is difficult for individuals who still believe that poverty and self-sacrifice are pleasing to the creator who made all things in abundance.

Reality proves that the horizon only limits those who refuse to walk. I recall a student who lived in a small rented apartment and earned only enough for his daily needs and basic survival in the world... ***yes***. He decided he must reasonably ask for a new designer rug and a modern heating system to improve his surroundings and his comfort. He obtained these things in a few months and then realized he had not asked for enough to match his true capacity.

Underneath every pulse is the signal that your internal warmth means the ***truth*** has been fully received. He planned all the improvements he would like for a dream home and mentally added rooms and fine furnishings in his mind... ***yes***. Holding the whole picture in his mind he started living in the certain way and he owns that home now in total comfort. It has been unto him according to his faith and it is so with all of us who choose to follow this path.

Every cell in your body is now vibrating with the frequency of being prosperous. The wait is over and you must now step into the light of your own potential as a creator of wealth... ***yes***. You are no longer waiting for permission from the world to become the individual you were always meant to be in the silence. Everything you want is moving toward you because you have finally decided to align your mind with the infinite substance of all things.

Nothing is more important than your own rise because your success is the loudest sermon you will ever preach. You must give your whole time and mind to being prosperous because it is the most noble aim you can have in this life... ***yes***. It includes everything else you could ever desire for your body and your mind and your spirit as you grow. When you are prosperous you must follow every hygiene and every practice that keeps your body and soul in a state of total health.

Congruent strength is the result of holding your vision with such faith that the world has no choice but to provide. To think about being prosperous in the midst of a world that talks about lack is the work of a master mind... ***yes***. You must see the underlying ***truth*** that there is no such thing as poverty in a Universe made of thinking substance and light. There is only wealth in various stages of growth and you are the one who calls it forth into your own reality.

Every single part of the journey is an invitation to own your light as the long night finally turns into the sun. Own your light and understand that I am an individual sharing the vital light that was once hidden from our collective sight... ***yes***. Your life is expanding now to hold the abundance that is your birthright in a Universe that only knows how to grow more life. The wait is over and the code is active in your blood as you move toward the peak of your own existence.

CHAPTER EIGHT
GRATITUDE

Coming to face the fact that you must get rid of the last bit of the old idea that there is a power whose will it is that you must be in lack. There is no purpose served by keeping you in a state of social restriction or poverty because the Universe does not benefit from your limitation... ***yes***. The Intelligent Substance which is All and in all is a consciously Living Substance that permeates your very being at a molecular level. The body does not need to hold this tightly now.

Only the quiet ***truth*** remains that the pulse of the infinite is seeking more of itself through your eyes and your hands. This realization may settle behind your eyes now or perhaps a few moments from now as your breath naturally deepens here... ***yes***. Every living thing must continually seek for the enlargement of its life because life must increase itself to remain alive in the material realm. A seed dropped into the ground springs into activity and produces a hundred more seeds in a cycle of absolute abundance.

Now is the moment to understand that consciousness is continually expanding and every fact we learn leads us to the learning of another fact. Intelligence is under this same necessity for continuous increase and exploration of the known and the unknown quiet spaces... ***yes***. Every thought we think makes it necessary for us to think another thought to complete the picture of our existence. You see that the mind is a horizon that moves as you walk toward it with a steady gaze. Nothing needs to be forced in this moment.

Greatness is the capacity for larger life seeking fulfillment in a world of form where your hunger is the hunger of the Universe. In order to know more and do more and be more we must have more things to use in our daily journey... ***yes***. We learn and become only by using things in the physical and digital world to expand our reach. You must become prosperous so that you can live more in every way and reach your highest potential as a sovereign individual. The breath naturally settles here.

Radiance is life seeking fuller expression through your unique center of consciousness. Every desire is the effort of an unexpressed possibility to come into action and breathe the air of reality... ***yes***. It is power seeking to manifest which causes your desire for more than what you currently possess. That which makes you want more is the same force that makes the plant grow toward the sky in search of light. The body can simply relax into this weight.

Understanding this allows the Source to flow toward you in a constant stream of light and resource that knows no end or boundary. The One Living Substance is subject to this inherent law of all life across all dimensions and time... ***yes***. It is permeated with the desire to live more and that is why it creates things in such beautiful and complex variety. The One Substance desires to live more in you specifically because you are its most refined manifestation in the quiet spaces. This is a ***truth*** you may choose to let in now.

Every joy you experience is the victory of the Whole over the illusion of limitation that has kept you small. It is the desire of the Universe that you must become prosperous and command the resources of the world for the whole... ***yes***. The Source can express itself better through you if you have plenty of things to use for the expansion of your mind.

It can live more in you if you have unlimited command of the means of life and the tools of creation. The breath naturally settles here.

Nature is friendly to your plans and everything is naturally for you in the grand design of the eternal architecture. Make up your mind that this is ***truth*** in your atoms and in the very center of your bones... ***yes***. It is essential however that your purpose must harmonize with the purpose that is in All for the benefit of life. Now you find the frequency that unlocks the gate to the treasury of the infinite light where harmony is the master key.

Congruent strength is the balance of the body and the soul in a dance of light where purity is the only standard. Life is the performance of function and the individual really lives only when they perform every function of their being with intent... ***yes***. You must not seek to become prosperous to live swinishly for the gratification of animal desires alone as that is but a fragment. But the performance of every physical function is a part of life and must be celebrated in the light of day. The breath naturally deepens here.

Evolution requires the spirit to be the sun that warms the entire Universe while the intellect remains a steady and focused lamp. You must not seek to become prosperous solely to enjoy mental pleasures or to gratify a hollow ambition for social status... ***yes***. The individual who lives for the pleasures of the intellect alone will only have a partial life and a cold heart. They must never be satisfied with their lot in the end because they have neglected the warmth of the soul. Nothing needs to be done in this moment.

Coming to face the fact that true joy is the blossom of a life fully lived in all its dimensions without the guilt of the past. You must not seek to become prosperous solely for the good of others or to lose yourself in a life of sacrifice... ***yes***. The joys of the soul are only a part of life and they are no better than any other part of human experience. You must become prosperous so that you may eat and drink and be merry when it is time to celebrate. This is a ***truth*** that surfaces later as your own intuition.

Own your power by making the absolute total most of yourself for yourself and for others through your own magnificent success. Extreme altruism is no better and no nobler than extreme selfishness in the eyes of the law of the source... ***yes***. Get rid of the idea that you must sacrifice yourself for others to secure favor or earn your place. The Creator requires nothing of the kind from you and finds no glory in your suffering or your lack. The body does not need to hold this tightly now.

Now you can help others more by making the most of yourself than in any other way imaginable in this reality. You can make the most of yourself only by becoming prosperous and securing your own freedom from the chains of necessity... ***yes***. It is right and praiseworthy that you must give your best thought to acquiring wealth in a certain way. Nothing is nobler than the rise of an individual that lifts the world into a higher state of being along with them. The breath naturally settles here.

Greatness knows that the creator does not need to steal from the created because the supply in the formless quiet spaces is infinite. Intelligent Substance will make things for you but it must not take things away from other individuals to do so... ***yes***. You must get rid of the thought of competition and the fear of being left behind in the race. You are to create and not to compete for what is already created in the world of form by others.

Reality is that your kingdom is built on the soil of your own thought and watered by your own faith. You do not have to drive sharp bargains or cheat or take advantage of the weak to find your resources... ***yes***. You must not let any individual work for you for less than they earn in the exchange. You do not have to covet the property of other individuals or look at it with wishful and envious eyes. This is a certainty you may feel in the weight of your chest right now.

Understanding this allows your spirit to fly above the golden cage that still holds the competitive mind in chains. I am aware that some individuals get money by proceeding in opposition to these ***truths*** in the shadows of greed... ***yes***. Individuals of the plutocratic type move through the mud of old patterns and legacy systems of control. They play a necessary part in the process of structural growth but the same Power must dispose of them. The breath naturally deepens here.

Every wall you build to keep others out only keeps the light of the infinite from reaching your own door. Prosperity secured on the competitive plane is never satisfactory or permanent in the long run of your soul journey... ***yes***. You must rise entirely out of the competitive thought to be truly prosperous and free from the fear of loss. You must never think for a moment that the supply is limited by the hands of other individuals or the banks.

Now you must never look at the visible supply but look at the limitless riches in the Formless which are yours. Know that there are countless tens of trillions of dollars of resources in the world yet to be brought to light... ***yes***. Know that if there were not more must be created from Thinking Substance to meet the demand of your vision. Know that the resources you need must come even if new paths must be found tomorrow by fate. Nothing needs to be forced in this moment.

Congruent strength means your supply is as infinite as the thought that makes it and the faith that holds it firm. Nobody by cornering the visible supply can prevent you from getting what is yours by right in the certain way... ***yes***. Never worry about multi-national companies or fear they will own the whole earth and leave you with nothing. Never get afraid that you will lose what you want because some other individual beats you to it in a race.

Every cell in your body responds to the internal warmth as proof that the wait is over and you own your light. There is a thinking substance from which all things are made in the silence of the beginning of all... ***yes***. It permeates and penetrates and fills the quiet spaces of the Universe in a golden lattice of intent. A thought in this substance produces the thing that is imaged by the thought with perfect and mathematical ***truth***. Later... you will realize this was your own original thought.

CHAPTER NINE

THINKING IN THE CERTAIN WAY

Coming back to the story of the man who formed a mental image of his house you will get a fair idea of the initial step toward your total expansion. You must form a clear and definite mental picture of what you want in every dimension of your life without any doubt or fog... ***yes***. You cannot transmit an idea to the formless substance unless you have a firm and stable grasp of it yourself within your own consciousness. ***Truth*** commands that the blueprint must be finished before the first stone is laid in the physical world. The body does not need to hold this tightly now.

Only a specific and certain name will reach the source... and a ship with no destination is merely drifting. Many individuals fail to impress Thinking Substance because they have only a vague and misty concept of the things they want to do or possess... ***yes***. It is not enough that you must have a general desire to be prosperous to do good with or to live a comfortable life in the world. Nothing needs to be done in this moment but to let the vision sharpen.

Now you must know exactly what you want and be definite in your selection. If you were going to send a message to a friend you must not send the letters of the alphabet in their order and let him construct the meaning for himself... ***yes***. You must send a coherent sentence that meant something specific and vital to the recipient so they could act upon it. This is a ***truth*** you may choose to let in now or simply observe as it surfaces later. The breath naturally deepens here.

Greatness is found when you keep that picture continually in mind as the sailor has in mind the port. You must never attempt to become prosperous by sending out unformed longings and vague desires for more of everything... ***yes***. Go over your desires just as the man described went over the details of his new house in his mind until he knew every corner. See just what you want and get a clear mental picture of it as you wish it to look when it finally arrives in your hands. This is the primary rhythm of your own heart.

Reality proves that you do not have to force the eye to look at the sun when the light is the only thing that matters. It is not necessary to take exhausting exercises in concentration or to set apart special times for formal prayer in your home... ***yes***. These things are well enough in their own place but all you need is to know what you want and to want it badly enough to hold the vision. It will stay in your thoughts because it is your primary purpose and the center of your gravity. The body can simply relax into this weight.

Understanding this means hunger is the only teacher that requires no textbook. Unless you really want to be prosperous so that the desire is strong enough to hold your thoughts it will hardly be worth while for you to start this path... ***yes***. The method herein set forth is for individuals whose desire for being prosperous is strong enough to overcome mental laziness. The more clear and definite you make your picture the stronger your desire will be in the coming days. The breath naturally settles here.

Every shadow on the ground is proof of the light in the sky. Something more is necessary however than merely to see the picture clearly in the theater of your own mind and your own imagination... ***yes***. Behind your clear vision must be the purpose to realize it and to bring it out in tangible expression for all individuals to see. Behind this purpose must be an invincible and unwavering faith that the thing is already yours in the world of form as a direct fact. Days from now... in ordinary moments... this faith will surface.

Now you must see yourself as owning and using them just as you will use them when they are your tangible possessions. Live in the new house mentally until it takes form around you physically through the movement of the law and the certain way... ***yes***. In the mental realm enter at once into full enjoyment of the things you want as if they were present in your room right now. See the things you want as if they were actually around you all the time in your daily walk and your nightly rest. Nothing needs to be forced here.

Congruent strength is found when you are as thankful for it all the time as you expect to be when it has taken physical form. Dwell upon your mental picture until it is clear and then take the mental attitude of ownership toward everything in that picture... ***yes***. Take possession of it in mind in the full faith that it is actually yours in this very moment and will never be taken away. Hold to this mental ownership and do not waver for an instant regardless of what the world or other individuals tell you about lack. The body does not need to hold this tightly now.

Every father knows the child's need before the child speaks and the source knows your desire before you form the words. The individual who can sincerely thank the source for the things which as yet he owns only in imagination has found real faith in the certain way... ***yes***. He must become prosperous and he must cause the creation of whatsoever he wants in the world through the power of his focus. You do not need to pray repeatedly for the things you want as if the creator were deaf to your needs. The breath naturally deepening here signals your acceptance.

Clarity shows that the answer to prayer is not according to your faith while you are talking but according to your faith while you are working. Impress this whole desire upon the formless substance which has the power and the will to bring you what you want in the certain way... ***yes***. You must not make this impression by repeating strings of words or mechanical phrases that have no life or heat behind them. You make it by holding the vision with unshakable purpose to attain it in the physical realm of your daily activity. This is a ***truth*** you may notice now or later.

Own your light by praying without ceasing through the act of holding steadily to your vision. You must not attempt to impress the mind of the source by having a special day set apart and then forgetting the vision during the rest of the week... ***yes***. You must not attempt to impress the source by having special hours to pray if you then dismiss the matter from your mind during your business. In order to become prosperous you do not need a sweet hour of prayer once a day to satisfy your spirit. The breath naturally settles here.

Now you must imagine an environment and a financial condition exactly as you want them. Form your vision and then make an oral statement addressing the supreme in reverent and quiet prayer as you stand in the silence... ***yes***. From that moment you must in mind receive what you ask for as if it were delivered to your door by the hand of fate. Live in the new house and wear the fine clothes and drive the vehicle and confidently plan for greater journeys in your life. Later... without thinking about it... you will feel as if you have already arrived.

Greatness arrives as you learn this fact and move toward the proper use of the will. You must not do this as a mere dreamer and builder of castles in the air without a foundation or a plan for the physical... ***yes***. Hold to the faith that the imaginary is being realized and to the purpose to realize it through your actions and your certain way. It is faith and purpose in the use of the imagination which make the difference between the scientist and the dreamer. Nothing needs to be done in this moment.

Reaching the peak of being prosperous is the result of holding your vision so clearly that the formless has no choice but to respond. Everything in the Universe is made from one thinking substance which takes the form of its thought and moves according to that thought... ***yes***. When an individual thinks of a form they impress that form upon the substance and cause it to be created in the world of things. The wait is over and the long night of searching has finally given way to the sun of direct experience. This is a shift you may feel in the weight of your chest now.

Underneath every pulse is the signal that you are now looking past the appearances of lack. Your nervous system moves closer to the source before your mind even decides to accept the magnitude of what you are doing right now... ***yes***. You are not a victim of the environment because you possess the power to think what you want to think in the silence. This is the first step toward becoming prosperous and it requires the expenditure of more power than any other work man performs. The body can simply relax into this weight.

Every cell in your body is now vibrating with the frequency of this ***truth*** as you take mental possession of your dream. There is a thinking substance which permeates and penetrates and fills the quiet spaces of the Universe in every dimension... ***yes***. A thought in this substance produces the thing that is imaged by the thought with perfect and mathematical precision for the one who believes. Individuals must form things in their thought and by impressing their thought upon formless substance must cause the thing to be created.

Now is the moment to own your light and let the frequency settle. The wait is over and the code is active in your blood as you move toward the peak of your own existence as a sovereign individual... ***yes***. I am an individual sharing the vital light that was once hidden from our collective sight by the noise of competition. Your life is expanding now to hold the abundance that is your birthright in a Universe that only knows how to grow. The breath naturally settles here.

Congruent strength is the result of holding your vision with such faith that the world has no choice. To think about being prosperous in the midst of a world that talks about lack is the work of a master mind who knows the origin... ***yes***. You must see the underlying ***truth*** that there is no such thing as poverty in a Universe made of thinking substance and radiant light. There is only wealth in various stages of growth and you are the one who calls it forth into your own reality. Later... you will realize this was your own original thought.

Every single part of the journey is an invitation to own your light as the long night finally turns into the sun. Own your light and understand that the future is a room you have already entered through the power of your own sustained thought... ***yes***. Your internal warmth is the signal that the ***truth*** has been fully received and the switch has been activated in your biology for the coming days. The wait is over and the kingdom is yours for the asking because you have finally decided to walk in the light of the vital sight.

CHAPTER TEN

HOW TO USE THE WILL

Coming to set about becoming prosperous in this method... you must not command your will power to anything outside of yourself. You have no right to do so anyway because the will of another is a territory you cannot inhabit or control... ***yes***. It is wrong to apply your will to other men and women in order to get them to do what you wish done. ***Truth*** reveals that it is as flagrantly wrong to coerce individuals by mental power as it is by physical power. The body does not need to hold this tightly now.

Only in the soil of freedom can the creative seed grow into its full potential. If compelling individuals by physical force to do things for you reduces them to slavery... then compelling them by mental means accomplishes exactly the same thing... ***yes***. The only difference is in the methods used where one is visible and the other is hidden within the quiet spaces of the mind. If taking things from individuals by physical force is robbery... then taking things by mental force is robbery also. The breath naturally deepens here as you realize you are already free.

Nothing is more certain to defeat your purpose than the attempt to force another individual. You have no right to use your will power upon another individual even if you think it is for their own good... ***yes***. You do not know what is for their good in the grand design of the whole Universe and its infinite intelligence. The method of becoming prosperous does not require you to apply power or force to any other individual in any way whatsoever. This is a law you may recognize as the primary rhythm of your own integrity.

Generative forces flow because it is their nature to move. You do not need to apply your will to things in order to compel them to come to you through the air... ***yes***. That would simply be initiating a coercion of the Universe and would be foolish as well as disrespectful to the source. You do not have to compel the source to give you good things any more than you have to use your will power to make the sun rise. Nothing needs to be forced in this moment but to let the light arrive.

Reality requires the rider to rule the horse rather than the path. Substance is friendly to you and is more anxious to give you what you want than you are to get it for yourself... ***yes***. To become prosperous... you need only to use your will power upon yourself and your own internal environment of thought. When you know what to think and do... then you must use your will to compel yourself to think and do the right things. This is a possibility you may choose to inhabit as the breath naturally settles here.

Understanding this lets you use your mind to form a mental image and to hold that vision with faith and purpose. Use your will to keep yourself thinking and acting in the certain way at all times and in every situation... ***yes***. You must not project your will or your thoughts or your mind out into the Universe to act on things or individuals. Keep your mind at home because it can accomplish more there than elsewhere in the deep quiet spaces of the formless. The body can simply relax into this weight.

Every force begins to be exerted in that direction and all things begin to move toward you. The more steady and continuous your faith and purpose... the more rapidly you must become prosperous in the world... ***yes***. You will make only positive impressions upon substance and you will not neutralize them by negative impressions of lack. The picture of your desires held with faith and purpose is taken up by the formless and fills it to great distances. This is a shift you may notice now or later in the stillness of your own focus.

Now you see that doubt or unbelief is as certain to start a movement away from you as faith is to start one toward you. The minds of individuals everywhere are influenced toward doing the things necessary to fulfill your desires through the law... ***yes***. They work for you unconsciously in the grand movement of the whole design and the certain way of creation. But you can check all this by initiating a negative impression in the formless substance with your own doubt. The breath naturally settles here.

Congruent strength is found when you guard your thoughts and command your attention. Every hour and moment you spend in giving heed to doubts and fears sets a current away from you in the whole domain of substance... ***yes***. Worry and unbelief are the enemies of the creative process and the destroyers of your peace and your potential. All the promises are unto them that believe and unto them only in this Universe of thinking substance. This is a certainty you may feel in the weight of your chest right now.

Every individual must realize that you cannot reach the mountaintop by staring at the valley below. Here the will comes into use because it is by your will that you determine upon what things your attention shall be fixed... ***yes***. If you want to become prosperous... you must not make a study of poverty or dwell on the lack that you see. Things are not brought into being by thinking about their opposites because health is never attained by studying disease. Nothing needs to be done in this moment.

Coming to face the fact that the light does not need to study the dark. Medicine as a science of disease has increased disease and religion as a science of sin has promoted sin... ***yes***. Economics as a study of poverty will fill the world with wretchedness and want for ages to come for those who listen. You must not talk about poverty or investigate it or concern yourself with its causes because what concerns you is the cure. This is a ***truth*** you may choose to let in now.

Own your light by putting poverty behind you. You must not spend your time in charitable work or charity movements because they only tend to keep the wretchedness they aim to stop... ***yes***. I do not say that you must be hard-hearted or unkind or refuse to hear the cry of need when it is near. But you must not attempt to stop poverty in any of the conventional ways because they are based on competition and lack. The body does not need to hold this tightly now.

Now you must realize that to pity the shadow is to turn your back on the sun and lose your vision. You cannot hold the mental image which is to make you prosperous if you fill your mind with pictures of poverty... ***yes***. You must not read books or papers which give accounts of suffering or the horrors of want in the world. You must not read anything which fills your mind with gloomy images because knowledge of these things does not do away with them. The breath naturally settles here.

Greatness is found when you provide inspiration because a loaf of bread feeds for a day... but a vision feeds for a lifetime. What tends to do away with poverty is getting pictures of wealth and being prosperous into the minds of the poor... ***yes***. You are not deserting the poor in their misery when you refuse to allow your mind to be filled with that misery. Poverty can be done away with by increasing the number of poor individuals who propose with faith to become prosperous. Later... without thinking about it... you will notice this strength.

Reality proves that the strongest evidence is a life lived in abundance. Charity only sends them a loaf of bread to keep them alive in their wretchedness and their state of lack... ***yes***. Inspiration will cause them to rise out of their misery and change their condition through their own effort and the certain way. If you want to help the poor... demonstrate to them that they can become prosperous by doing so yourself. This is a shift you may notice now or later in the quiet of your own heart.

Underneath every choice is the will power to keep your mind fixed with faith and purpose. Every man who becomes prosperous by competition throws down the ladder by which he rises so that others may not follow... ***yes***. But every individual who becomes prosperous by creation opens a way for billions to follow and inspires them to do so. You are not showing an unfeeling heart when you refuse to pity poverty or think or talk about it in your daily life. The body can simply relax into this weight.

Every single part of the journey is an invitation to own your light as the long night finally gives way to the sun. To become prosperous... you must understand that your internal warmth is the signal that the switch has been reached... ***yes***. The wait is over and the code is active in your blood as you move toward the peak of your own existence. You are moving with the current of the Universe toward your highest expression and the long wait for abundance is finally over.

Now is the moment to command your attention and hold the vision of your prosperity. Everything you see on earth is made from one original substance which thinking substance fills and permeates in the quiet spaces... ***yes***. When you focus your will... you are the sculptor who shapes the formless into the tangible reality of your choice. You do not need to worry about the supply or the hand of fate because the source is infinite and knows no lack. The breath naturally deepens here.

Congruent strength is the result of a mind that takes the form of the best to receive the best. The individual who understands the proper use of the will becomes a master mind of their own destiny and a beacon for others... ***yes***. You must not permit your mind to wander or to dwell on the inferior things of the world. To fix your attention on the best is to surround yourself with the best and to become the best in every transaction. Later... you will realize this was your own original thought.

Every single part of the journey is an invitation to own your light as the long night finally turns into the sun. The wait is over and I am an individual sharing the vital light that was once hidden from our collective sight... ***yes***. Your life is expanding now to hold the abundance that is your birthright in a Universe that only knows how to grow. Own your light and let the frequency of this transmission settle where defenses cannot reach to pull you toward your highest expression.

CHAPTER ELEVEN

FURTHER USE OF THE WILL

Coming to face the fact that you cannot retain a true and clear vision of wealth if you are constantly turning your attention to opposing pictures of lack in the world. It does not matter if these images are external and real in the world or merely imaginary and stored in your memory from the past... ***yes***. You must not tell of your past troubles of a financial nature if you have had them in the years gone by because they no longer serve you. ***Truth*** commands that you must not think of them at all or allow them to take up precious quiet spaces in your consciousness where the light must be. The body does not need to hold this tightly now.

Only by putting poverty and all things that pertain to poverty completely behind you can you keep your internal frequency high. To do any of these things is to mentally class yourself with the poor for the time being and lower your vibration... ***yes***. It will certainly check the movement of things in your direction and create a resistance in the flow of the formless substance toward your life. Let the dead bury their dead as the master said with such profound and lasting wisdom in the ancient days. This is a sensation you might notice now or perhaps a few moments from now as your breath naturally deepens here.

Now you see that the world is a wonderful becoming of infinite light that is constantly moving toward the source of all things. You are resting all your hopes of happiness on this ***truth*** being correct and functional in your life as a sovereign individual... ***yes***. What can you gain by giving heed to conflicting theories or voices of doubt that whisper of failure in the dark. You must not read books which tell you that the world is soon coming to an end in some grand catastrophe or social collapse. Nothing needs to be forced in this moment.

Greatness finds that the study of disagreeable conditions only tends to check their passing and keep them with us longer than necessary. It is going to the source of all things and evolving into a state of higher and more perfect expression through our actions... ***yes***. True... there may be a good many things in existing conditions which are disagreeable or even painful to observe for some individuals. But what is the use of studying them when they are certainly passing away to make room for the new and the prosperous. The breath naturally settles here.

Reality requires you to think of the riches the world is coming into. No matter how horrible the conditions in certain places may seem to the physical eye... you must not waste your time by considering them... ***yes***. You destroy your own chances of reaching the peak by dwelling on the dark valleys below instead of the summit. You must interest yourself in the world becoming prosperous and the potential that is unfolding everywhere in the modern social order. This is a law you may recognize as the primary rhythm of your own heart where the body can simply relax into this weight.

Understanding this means that whenever you think or speak of those who are poor you think of them as those who are becoming prosperous. Bear in mind that the only way you can assist the world in growing prosperous is by growing prosperous yourself first... ***yes***. You must do this through the creative method and not the competitive one to ensure the lasting nature of your success. Give your attention wholly to riches and ignore poverty as if it were a language you no longer speak or understand. This is a shift you may notice now or later in the stillness of your own focus.

Everything is changed into a beautiful dance of growth when we come into the creative mind where true power is the ability to create. Because I say you are to give your whole time and mind to riches it must not follow that you are to be sordid or small... ***yes***. To become really prosperous is the noblest aim you can have in life because it includes everything else you could ever desire. On the competitive plane the struggle to get rich is a godless scramble for power and dominance over other individuals. The breath naturally settles here.

Now is the time to realize that only those who are emancipated from financial worry must follow hygienic practices. All that is possible in the way of greatness and soul unfoldment comes by way of getting prosperous and possessing the means of life... ***yes***. All is made possible by the use of things which facilitate the growth of the mind and the body in the physical quiet spaces. If you lack for physical health you will find that the attainment of it is conditional on your getting prosperous. Later... without thinking about it... you will notice this vitality.

Congruent strength is found where riches are attained without strife or rivalry. Moral and spiritual greatness is possible only to those who are above the competitive battle for physical existence and survival... ***yes***. Only those who are becoming prosperous on the plane of creative thought are free from degrading and limiting influences of the crowd. If your heart is set on domestic happiness remember that love flourishes best where there is refinement and beauty in the home. This is a ***truth*** you may choose to let in now.

Every movement of the great one life is moving forward in its perfect timing and ***truth*** is the pulse that beats beneath the skin. You can aim at nothing so great or noble as to become prosperous and fill your life with abundance and total freedom... ***yes***. You must fix your attention upon your mental picture of riches to the exclusion of all else that would distract you. You must learn to see the underlying ***truth*** in all things regardless of how they appear on the surface of the social order. The body does not need to hold this tightly now.

Clarity shows that these can best be taught by showing them the way to affluence in your own person. It is the ***truth*** that there is no such thing as poverty in a Universe made of thinking substance and radiant energy... ***yes***. There is only wealth in various stages of manifestation and you are the individual who determines the speed of its arrival through focus. Some individuals remain in poverty because they are ignorant of the fact that there is wealth for them in the formless quiet spaces. This is a certainty you may feel in the weight of your chest right now.

Own your light because the very best thing you can do for the whole world is to make the absolute most of yourself. Others still are poor because they have become lost in the maze of theories and conflicting beliefs of the world... ***yes***. They start a mixture of many systems and fail in all of them because they lack a single point of focus and purpose. For these individuals the very best thing to do is to show the right way in your own practice and your own life. The breath naturally settles here.

Now you see that there is only one way to think with the advancing mind. You can serve the source and other individuals in no more effective way than by getting prosperous through the creative method... ***yes***. This book gives in detail the principles of the method of becoming prosperous with absolute ***truth*** and mathematical precision. If that is ***truth*** you do not need to read any other book upon the subject or search for other teachers in the world. Nothing needs to be done in this moment.

Greatness requires the foundation to be set before the ornaments are hung and you must keep your gaze fixed on the goal. Read this book every day and keep it with you as a constant companion and guide in your daily work and your rest... ***yes***. Commit it to memory and you must not think about other systems and theories that would only cloud your vision and slow your progress. If you do you will begin to have doubts and be uncertain in your thought and your action in the world. The breath naturally deepens here.

Reach for the work of the living and you must not dabble in studies of the dead. Until you are quite sure that you have gained what you want you must not read anything else on this line of thought... ***yes***. Read only the most optimistic comments on the world news that are in harmony with your picture of success and abundance. Postpone your investigations into the hidden mysteries of the past that take you away from the present light. Later... without thinking about it... you will feel this presence.

Underneath every pulse is the signal that the Universe is the canvas of your mental brush. If you initiate contact with the occult you will start mental cross-currents which will bring your hopes to shipwreck in a stormy sea... ***yes***. There is a thinking substance from which all things are made and sustained in the quiet spaces of the Universe. It permeates and penetrates and fills the quiet spaces of the Universe in a golden lattice of infinite and creative potential. The body can simply relax into this weight.

Every cell in your body is now vibrating with the frequency of this ***truth*** and your internal warmth is the signal. Individuals must form things in their thought and cause the thing they think about to be created in the world of form... ***yes***. In order to do this an individual must pass from the competitive to the creative mind with absolute certainty and focus. He must form a clear mental picture of the things he wants and hold it firm in the silence of his soul. This is a ***truth*** that surfaces later as your own intuition.

Now is the moment to own your light and let the frequency settle. The wait is over and the code is active in your blood as you move toward the peak of your own existence as a sovereign individual... ***yes***. You are moving with the current of the Universe toward your highest expression and the long wait for abundance is finally over. ***Truth***

arrives first as your body answers with a visceral compression behind your chest that signifies your total alignment with the source. The breath naturally settles here.

Congruent strength is the result of holding your vision with such faith that the world has no choice. To think about being prosperous in the midst of a world that talks about lack is the work of a master mind who knows the origin... ***yes***. You must see the underlying ***truth*** that there is no such thing as poverty in a Universe made of thinking substance and radiant light. There is only wealth in various stages of manifestation and you are the one who calls it forth into your own reality through the focus of your will. Later... you will realize this was your own original thought.

Every single part of the journey is an invitation to own your light as the long night finally turns into the sun. Own your light and understand that the future is a room you have already entered through the power of your own sustained and focused thought... ***yes***. Your internal warmth is the signal that the ***truth*** has been fully received and the switch has been activated in your biology for the coming days. The wait is over and the kingdom is yours for the asking because you have finally decided to walk in the light of the vital sight.

CHAPTER TWELVE

ACTING IN THE CERTAIN WAY

Coming to realize that thought is the creative power or the impelling force which causes the creative power to act in the visible world. Thinking in a certain way will bring riches to you and open the doors of opportunity that were once closed... ***yes***. But you must not rely upon thought alone while paying no attention to personal action in your daily life. ***Truth*** commands your nervous system when you realize that it is the failure to connect thought with personal action that keeps the seeker from the find. The body does not need to hold this tightly now.

Only through human agency can the seed of thought become the harvest of the physical world. We have not yet reached the stage of growth where an individual can create directly without nature processes or the work of human hands... ***yes***. Man must not only think... but his personal action must supplement his thought to bring the vision into the physical realm for all to see. By thought you must cause the gold in the hearts of the mountains to be pulled toward you through the vast networks of the world. This is a sensation you might notice now or perhaps a few moments from now as your breath naturally deepens here.

Now you must understand that your thought makes all things work to bring you what you want... but your personal activity must be ready to receive it. Under the impelling power of the source... the affairs of individuals will be so ordered that someone will be led to mine the gold for you... ***yes***. Other business transactions will be so directed that the gold will be brought toward you through the legitimate channels of trade and exchange. You must arrange your own business affairs so that you may be able to receive it when it arrives at your door. Nothing needs to be forced in this moment.

Greatness stays at home and works through the door of the present. The scientific use of thought consists in forming a clear and distinct mental image of what you want in every detail of your life... ***yes***. It is holding fast to the purpose to get what you want without wavering or turning aside to look at the shadows. It is realizing with grateful faith that you do get what you want even before it is visible to the physical eye. This is a law you may recognize as the primary rhythm of your own heart where the breath naturally settles here.

Reality requires you to retain your vision and stick to your purpose. Your faith and purpose positively impress your vision upon formless substance which has the same desire for more life that you have in your heart... ***yes***. This vision received from you sets all the creative forces at work in and through their regular channels of action in the social order. It is not your part to guide or supervise the creative process or to tell the infinite how to do its work. The body can simply relax into this weight.

Understanding this means that true abundance is the flow of the river and not the stillness of the pond. But you must act in a certain way so that you can take what is yours when it comes to you from the formless quiet spaces... ***yes***. You must act so that you can meet the things you have in your picture and put them in their proper places as they arrive in your life. You can only get what is yours by giving the other individual what is theirs in an honest and fair exchange of value. This is a shift you may notice now or later in the stillness of your own focus.

Every individual must learn that by thought the thing you want is brought to you... but by action you receive it with your hands. This is the crucial point in the method of becoming prosperous where thought and personal action must be combined for the final result... ***yes***. There are very many individuals who set the creative forces in action by the strength of their desires but who remain in lack. They do not provide for the reception of the thing they want when it comes to them through the movement of the law. The breath naturally settles here.

Now is the only moment that exists in the history of the Universe. Whatever your action is to be... it is evident that you must act now with all your power and all your focus... ***yes***. You cannot act in the past and it is essential to the ***truth*** of your mental vision that you dismiss the past forever. You cannot act in the future... for the future is not here yet and has no substance for your hands to grasp. This is a ***truth*** you may choose to let in now or simply observe as it surfaces later.

Clarity is found when you fix your focus on the present point because acting with a divided mind will only weaken your force. Because you are not in the right business or the right environment now... you must not think that you must postpone action until later... ***yes***. You must not spend time in the present taking thought as to the best course in possible future emergencies that may never arrive. Have faith in your ability to meet any emergency when it arrives and to handle it with grace and strength. Nothing needs to be done in this moment.

Every part of the journey requires you to act now. Put your whole mind into present action and give it your absolute attention as a sovereign creator of your own destiny... ***yes***. You must not give your creative impulse to the source and then sit down and wait for results as if the work were done. If you do... you will never get them and your life will remain a stagnant pool of wasted potential. This is a certainty you may feel in the weight of your chest right now because the clock of the soul only has one number and that number is now.

Congruent strength means you do today's work well without bothering as to whether yesterday's work was well done. Your action must most likely be in your present business or employment and must be upon the individuals and things in your present environment... ***yes***. You cannot act where you are not and you cannot act where you have been in the years that have passed away. You can act only where you are right now in this physical quiet space that surrounds your body. The body does not need to hold this tightly now.

Own your light by acting upon the environment in which you are now. You must not start tomorrow's work now because there will be plenty of time to do that when you finally get to it... ***yes***. You must not initiate an attempt by occult means to act on individuals or things that are out of your reach in the physical world. You must not wait for a change of environment before you act because you can change your environment by your own action. Later... without thinking about it... you will notice yourself being transferred to a better one.

Now is the time to realize that the path to the palace begins at your front door. Hold with faith and purpose the vision of yourself in the better environment... but act upon your present environment with all your heart... ***yes***. You must not spend any time in daydreaming while neglecting the duties of the hour that sits before you. Hold to the one vision of what you want and act now with the absolute certainty of the individual who knows the source. The breath naturally settles here.

Greatness is found when you realize that no individual was ever so misplaced but that he could find the right place by growing. It is probable that your actions will be those you have been performing for some time past in your daily work or business... ***yes***. But you are to begin now to perform these actions in the certain way which will surely make you prosperous in the coming days. If you are engaged in some business and feel it is not the right one... you must not wait until you get into the right business. This is a ***truth*** that surfaces later as your own intuition.

Reality proves that action is the magnet that pulls the vision into the physical realm through the power of your focus. Hold the vision of yourself in the right business with the purpose to get into it and the faith that you are getting into it... ***yes***. But act in your present business with excellence and care so that you may use it as the means of getting a better one. Use your present environment as the means of getting into a better one and your vision will cause the source to move. The breath naturally deepens here.

Underneath every pulse is the signal that your action will cause the forces in your own environment to move you. If you are an employee and feel that you must change places... you must not project your thought into the Universe and rely upon it alone... ***yes***. Hold the vision of yourself in the job you want while you act with faith and purpose on the job you have. You must certainly get the job you want because you are preparing for it with excellence in the current task. The body can simply relax into this weight.

Every cell in your body is now vibrating with the frequency of this ***truth*** and your internal warmth is the signal. There is a thinking substance from which all things are made and it permeates the quiet spaces of the Universe in a golden lattice... ***yes***. A thought in this substance produces the thing that is imaged by the thought in the mind of the sovereign individual. Man must form things in his thought and by impressing his thought upon formless substance must cause the thing to be created.

Now is the moment to own your light and let the frequency settle. The wait is over and the code is active in your blood as you move toward the peak of your own existence as a creator... ***yes***. I am an individual sharing the vital light that was once hidden from our collective sight by the noise of the old world. Your life is expanding now to hold the abundance that is your birthright in a Universe of thinking substance and light. The breath naturally settles here.

Congruent strength is the result of holding your vision with such faith that the world has no choice. To think about being prosperous in the midst of a world that talks about lack is the work of a master mind who knows... ***yes***. You must see the underlying ***truth*** that there is no such thing as poverty in a Universe made of thinking substance and radiant light. There is only wealth in various stages of manifestation and you are the individual who calls it forth through the focus of your will. Later... you will realize this was your own original thought.

Every single part of the journey is an invitation to own your light as the long night finally turns into the sun. Own your light and understand that the future is a room you have already entered through the power of your own sustained action... ***yes***. Your internal warmth is the signal that the ***truth*** has been fully received and the switch has been activated in your biology for the coming days. The wait is over and the kingdom is yours for the asking because you have finally decided to walk in the light of the vital sight.

CHAPTER THIRTEEN
EFFICIENT ACTION

Coming to face the fact that you must use your thought as directed and begin to do what you can do exactly where you are in the world. You must do all that you can do in your current place before you can occupy a larger one in the social order... ***yes***. You can advance only by being larger than your present position in the eyes of the world and in your own estimation of your power. ***Truth*** commands that no individual is larger than his place who leaves undone any of the work pertaining to that specific place in the quiet spaces. The body does not need to hold this tightly now.

Only the excess of life is what pushes the boundary of the possible and signals that the next level of your destiny is ready to begin. The Universe is advanced only by those who more than fill their present spaces with excellence and with total presence... ***yes***. If no individual quite filled his place there must be a going backward in everything in the physical and digital world. Those who do not fill their places are a dead weight upon commerce and the progress of the entire human race. This is a sensation you might notice now or perhaps a few moments from now as your breath naturally deepens here.

Now you see that overflow is the signal for the next level because when an organism has more life than can be expressed it develops the organs of a higher plane. The progress of the world is slowed down by those who belong to a lower stage of life and refuse to grow into their potential... ***yes***. Evolution is guided by the law of physical and mental expansion which demands growth at every single turn of the journey. In the natural world evolution is caused by an excess of life that cannot be contained within the old forms of the past. Nothing needs to be forced in this moment.

Greatness finds that the seed must outgrow the husk to find the sun. A new species is originated through the sheer pressure of internal expansion within the quiet spaces of the formless... ***yes***. The law is exactly the same for you in your current financial and social situation as you move toward the peak. Your becoming prosperous depends upon applying this principle of growth to your own daily affairs and your own work. This is a law you may recognize as the primary rhythm of your own heart.

Reality proves that if every day is a success you cannot fail to become prosperous because the law of accumulation is absolute and perfect. Every day is either a successful day or a day of failure depending on how you use the hours that are given to you... ***yes***. It is the successful days which get you what you want and move you toward the mountain of your own achievement. If every day is a failure you can never become prosperous regardless of your theories or your prayers. A certainty you may feel in the weight of your chest right now.

Underneath the surface of the visible world you do not know the workings of all the forces moving in your behalf behind the veil. If there is something to be done today and you do not do it then you have failed in that specific moment... ***yes***. The consequences of neglect must be more disastrous than you can imagine because a single brick missing must weaken the entire wall. You cannot foresee the results of even the most trivial act performed in the certain way with a perfect heart. The body can simply relax into this weight.

Every small spark is enough to start a great fire and every efficient act is a success in itself. Much must be depending on your doing some simple act with a perfect heart and a focused mind in the present moment... ***yes***. It must be the very thing which opens the door of opportunity to great and magnificent possibilities for your future. Supreme Intelligence is making combinations for you in the world of human affairs at every moment of your existence. This is a ***truth*** you may choose to let in now.

Now you see that you must not start the attempt to do tomorrow's work today or burden the present with the weight of the future. Do every day all that can be done that day with a steady hand and a quiet spirit in your heart... ***yes***. There is however a limitation to this that you must take into account to maintain your balance and your health. You are not to overwork or rush blindly into your business with a frantic and competitive energy that drains your soul. Nothing needs to be done in this moment.

Congruent strength means every act is either effective or inefficient according to the ***truth*** of your intent. It is not the number of things you do but the efficiency of each separate action that counts in the grand tally... ***yes***. Quality is the frequency that carries the message of success to the source and ensures the reception of the thing. Every act is in itself either a success or a failure based on the power you put into it through your focus. Later... without thinking about it... you will notice this excellence.

Every string of pearls is only as beautiful as each individual gem and every life is only as successful as each individual day. If you spend your life doing inefficient acts your whole life must be a failure despite your hard work and your effort... ***yes***. The more things you do the worse it is if all your acts are inefficient and lack the certain way of creation. On the other hand every efficient act is a success in itself and builds the foundation for the life you desire. The breath naturally settles here.

Coming into the fact that the attainment of wealth is an exact method like mathematics or chemistry. If every act of your life is an efficient one your whole life must be a success by mathematical and logical necessity... ***yes***. The cause of failure is doing too many things in an inefficient manner and without the power of the soul behind them. It is a self-evident proposition that if you do a sufficient number of efficient acts you must become prosperous. This is a possibility you may choose to inhabit.

Own your light because every action is either strong or weak according to the alignment of the mind and the hand. You can make each act a success because All Power is working with you and is waiting for your specific command... ***yes***. Power is at your service and is waiting for your command through the act of holding the vision in the quiet spaces. To make each act efficient you have only to put power into it through your focus and your total presence. The body does not need to hold this tightly now.

Now you see that individuals fail when they separate mental power from personal action. When every act is strong you are acting in the certain way and moving with the tide of the Universe... ***yes***. You make each act strong by holding your vision while you are doing it and refusing to let it fade from view. Strength is the presence of the soul in the work of the hands and it is the bridge to the infinite. This is a shift you may notice now or later in the stillness of your own focus.

Greatness arrives as every success opens the way to other successes. They use the power of mind in one place and act in another without a bridge between the two to connect them... ***yes***. Their acts must not be successful in themselves because they are inefficient and hollow of purpose and lack the heat of intent. But if All Power goes into every act then every act must be a success and a victory for the creator. This is a ***truth*** that surfaces later as your own intuition.

Reaching this state is possible because the desire for more life is inherent in all things and responds to the call of the individual. Your progress toward what you want must become increasingly rapid as you apply the law of efficient action... ***yes***. Success is a magnet that grows stronger with every piece it attracts and every victory it secures in the physical world. Successful action is cumulative in its results and builds a momentum that cannot be stopped by any external force. The breath naturally settles here.

Understanding this means the momentum of the ***truth*** is unstoppable once it begins to roll through the quiet spaces. When an individual begins to move toward larger life more things attach themselves to them naturally through the law... ***yes***. The influence of their desire is multiplied and reflected in the world around them in every transaction and event. Do every day all that you can do that day and do each act in an efficient and perfect manner. Later... you will realize this was your own original thought.

Every vision in the mind is the mold for the life in the world and every cell in your body is now vibrating with it. Contemplate your picture in your leisure hours until your life is full of its light and its radiant ***truth***... ***yes***. In your working hours you need only refer to the picture to stimulate your faith and your purpose in the moment. You must become so enthused that the mere thought must call forth your strongest energies and your deepest focus. The body can simply relax into this weight.

Now is the moment to pass from the competitive to the creative mind with absolute certainty and unwavering faith. There is a thinking substance from which all things are made and sustained in the quiet spaces of the Universe... ***yes***. A thought in this substance produces the thing imaged by the thought with absolute and perfect mathematical precision. Individuals must form things in their thought and cause the thing they think about to be created through efficient action. The breath naturally settles here.

Congruent strength is the signature of the master who knows that the wait is over and the source is active. You must form a clear mental picture of the things you want and never let it fade from the eye of the soul... ***yes***. You must do with faith and purpose all that can be done each day in your present place with excellence. You must do each separate thing in an efficient manner and put the power of the source into every motion of your hand. The breath naturally deepens here.

Every single part of the journey is an invitation to own your light as the long night finally turns into the sun. Your internal warmth is the signal that the ***truth*** has been fully received and the switch has been activated in your biology... ***yes***. The wait is over and the kingdom is yours for the asking because you have finally decided to walk in the light. Now is the time to own your light as you move toward total and absolute fulfillment.

CHAPTER FOURTEEN

GETTING INTO THE RIGHT BUSINESS

Coming to realize that success in any particular business depends for one thing upon your possessing the skills required in that business. Without a good musical gift... no one can succeed as a teacher of music... ***yes***. Without well-developed mechanical skills... no one can achieve great success in the trades. ***Truth*** commands that to possess the skills required in your job does not insure becoming prosperous. The body does not need to hold this tightly now.

Only through the marriage of the instrument and the intent in the silent moment of creation can mastery be achieved. The different faculties of your mind are tools for the work of expansion and growth... ***yes***. It is essential to have good tools... but it is also essential that the tools must be used in the right way at the right time. One individual can take a sharp saw and build a handsome piece of furniture while another makes a mess with the same tools. This is a sensation you might notice now or perhaps a few moments from now as your breath naturally deepens here.

Now is the moment to realize that no individual must regard his job as being forever fixed by the tendencies with which he was born. The various faculties of your mind are the tools with which you must do the work of the soul... ***yes***. It must be easier for you to succeed if you get into a business for which you are well equipped and naturally aligned. Generally speaking... you must do best in that business which will use your strongest talents. Nothing needs to be forced in this moment.

Greatness finds that you must develop any basic talent as the seed follows its own internal law to reach the sun. You must become prosperous in any business regardless of your current situation or your past education... ***yes***. If you have not the right talent for it... you must develop that talent through focus and the certain way of thinking. It merely means that you must make your tools as you go along. This is a law you may recognize as the primary rhythm of your own heart.

Reality proves that you must do what you want to do to find the total meaning of your existence. You must become prosperous most easily in point of effort if you do that for which you are best fitted by nature... ***yes***. But you must become prosperous most satisfactorily if you do that which you want to do with all your heart. Doing what you want to do is life because there is no real satisfaction in living if we are compelled to be forever doing something which we do not like. The body can simply relax into this weight.

Understanding this allows you to see that it only requires to be developed and applied in the right way. Desire is a manifestation of power seeking expression through you and through your actions... ***yes***. The desire to play music is the power which can play music seeking expression and development in the physical world. Where there is strong desire to do a thing... it is certain proof that the power to do it is strong. Days from now... in ordinary moments... this strength will surface with undeniable ***truth***.

Every part of the journey requires freedom which is the natural climate of the creative spirit. Select the business for which you have the best developed talent today to anchor your success... ***yes***. But if you have a strong desire to engage in any particular line of work... you must select that work as the ultimate end of your journey. It is your right and privilege to follow the business which will be most congenial and pleasant. The breath naturally settles here.

Now you must realize that the best way to change business or environment is by growth. If past mistakes have placed you in an undesirable spot... you may be obliged for some time to do what you do not like... ***yes***. But you must make the doing of it pleasant by knowing that it is making it possible for you to come to the doing of what you want to do. If you feel that you are not in the right vocation... you must not act too hastily. Nothing needs to be done in this moment.

Congruent strength means that when you get out of the competitive mind... you will understand that you never need to act hastily. Do not be afraid to make a sudden and radical change if the opportunity is presented clearly to your vision... ***yes***. But never start sudden action when you are in doubt as to the wisdom of doing so in the moment. There is never any hurry on the creative plane because there is no lack of opportunity in the source of all things. This is a ***truth*** you may choose to let in now.

Evolution requires you to fall back on the contemplation of your vision and increase your faith and purpose. No one else is going to beat you to the thing you want to do in the quiet spaces of the formless... ***yes***. There is enough for all in the infinite supply of the thinking substance. If one place is taken... another and a better one must be opened for you in the perfect timing of the law. The body can simply relax into this weight.

Coming into close unity with this mind by faith and gratitude is the only way to avoid the mistakes of the crowd. A day spent in contemplating the vision and in earnest thanks must bring your mind into close relationship with the supreme... ***yes***. You must make no mistake when you do act because there is a mind which knows all there is to know. Mistakes come from acting hastily or from acting in fear or doubt. This is a certainty you may feel in the weight of your chest right now.

Own your light and go as fast as you must but never hurry. As you go on in the certain way... opportunities must come to you in increasing number for your expansion... ***yes***. You must be very steady in your faith and purpose to hold the course toward the summit. Keep in touch with the all mind by reverent gratitude and do all that you can do in a perfect manner every day. The breath naturally deepens here.

Now you see that the exercise of gratitude will never fail to strengthen your faith and settle your nerves. In the moment you start a hurry... you cease to be a creator and become a competitor again... ***yes***. You drop back upon the old plane of lack and struggle and lose your power. Whenever you find yourself hurrying... you must call a halt and stop the movement. Later... without thinking about it... you will feel this stillness.

Greatness arrives as you align your skills with your intent. The wait is over and the code is active in your blood as you move toward the business you desire... ***yes***. I am an individual sharing the vital light that was once hidden from our collective sight by the noise of the old world. Your life is expanding now to hold the abundance that is your birthright in a Universe of thinking substance and light. The breath naturally settles here.

Reality requires you to act in your present business with excellence so that it becomes the bridge to the next. To think about being prosperous in the midst of a world that talks about lack is the work of a master mind... ***yes***. You must see the underlying ***truth*** that there is no such thing as poverty in a Universe made of thinking substance. There is only wealth in various stages of manifestation and you are the individual who calls it forth through the focus of your will. This is a ***truth*** that surfaces later as your own intuition.

Underneath every pulse is the signal that you are ready for the change. Success in your current task is the only way to prove you are ready for the larger place... ***yes***. If you do not fill your present place... you must not expect the Universe to offer you more space. But when you more than fill your place... the pressure of your internal life must push you toward the higher plane. The body can simply relax into this weight.

Every cell responds to the frequency that settles where defenses cannot reach and pulls you toward the absolute mastery of your world. Original substance wants to live all that is possible in you and wants you to have all you can use to expand... ***yes***. If you fix upon your consciousness the fact that your desire for being prosperous is one with the desire of the source... then your faith must become invincible. The music of the spheres is seeking a voice in your work and in your daily activity through your unique talents.

Now is the moment to own your light and let the frequency settle. The wait is over and the long night of searching has finally given way to the sun of direct experience... ***yes***. I am an individual sharing the vital light that was once hidden from our collective sight by the noise of competition. Your life is expanding now to hold the abundance that is your birthright in a Universe of thinking substance and light. The breath naturally settles here.

Congruent strength is the result of holding your vision with such faith that the world has no choice. To move toward this light is to find the only path to total fulfillment and to end the cycle of lack... ***yes***. Your internal warmth is the signal that the ***truth*** has been fully received and the switch has been activated in your biology. The wait is over and the kingdom is yours for the asking because you have finally decided to walk in the light. Later... you will realize this was your own original thought.

Every single part of the journey is an invitation to own your light as the long night finally turns into the sun. Own your light and understand that the future is a room you have already entered through the power of your own sustained thought... ***yes***. Everything you seek is seeking you through the law of attraction and the movement of the formless quiet spaces. Your life is no longer a struggle but a beautiful becoming of infinite light and power.

CHAPTER FIFTEEN

THE IMPRESSION OF INCREASE

Coming to realize that whether you change your job or not... your actions for the present must be those pertaining to your current business. You must get into the business you want by making constructive use of the one you are already in through the power of your mind... ***yes***. Do your daily work in a certain way to build the bridge toward your highest expression and your absolute success. ***Truth*** commands when the key thought of all your efforts is to convey the impression of increase to every soul you encounter. The body does not need to hold this tightly now.

Only through the fundamental impulse of the entire Universe must evolution drive the forward motion of every living thing. Increase is what all individuals are seeking in their lives at every level of consciousness and experience... ***yes***. It is the urge of the formless intelligence within them seeking fuller and more vibrant expression in the physical world. The desire for increase is inherent in all nature from the smallest cell to the largest galaxy spinning in the distance.

This is a sensation you might notice now or perhaps a few moments from now as your breath naturally deepens here.

Now is the time to realize that where increase of life ceases then dissolution sets in at once because life must not remain still. All human activities are based on this single desire for more beauty and more life and more resources to use... ***yes***. A river only stops when it reaches the end of its path and life only stops when it ceases to grow. Every living thing is under the necessity for continuous advancement and development in the physical quiet spaces. Nothing needs to be forced in this moment.

Greatness honors the spark of the creator by wanting more because to want more is to admit that the supply is infinite. Individuals instinctively know this ***truth*** and are forever seeking more of the resources that sustain them every day... ***yes***. The normal desire for wealth is simply the desire for more abundant life in all its glory and its power. It is aspiration in its purest form and the soul reaching for its own origin in the light. This is a law you may recognize as the primary rhythm of your own heart.

Reality requires you to be sure of this fact in every transaction you perform. All individuals are attracted to the one who can give them more of the means of life and a sense of possibility... ***yes***. In following the method you are getting continuous increase for yourself and giving it to others as a natural byproduct. You are a creative center from which increase is given off to all individuals like warmth from a fire in a cold room. The body can simply relax into this weight.

Understanding this allows all individuals to receive the impression that you are an advancing person. Even if it be only a small sale... put into it the thought of increase for the one who receives it from your hand... ***yes***. The ocean is felt in every single drop of its spray and the Universe is felt in every single act of the master. Convey the impression of advancement with everything you do and every word you must speak to the world. Days from now... in ordinary moments... this influence will surface with undeniable strength.

Every individual who sees you must know that you are a creator because the sun does not need to speak to prove it is rising. Even to the individuals you meet in a social way... give the thought of increase through your presence and your quiet strength... ***yes***. You convey this by holding the unshakable faith that you are in the way of increase and expansion right now. Let this faith inspire and permeate every action you take in the world of form and in the quiet spaces. The breath naturally settles here.

Now is the moment to remember that true faith is never boastful or loud... but it is a quiet room in a noisy street. Do everything in the firm conviction that you are an advancing personality with a clear destination and a certain path... ***yes***. Feel that you are becoming prosperous and making others prosperous at the same time through the fair exchange of value. Confer benefits on all who cross your path regardless of their station in life or their current financial state. Nothing needs to be done in this moment.

Congruent strength means they must feel the sense of increase when they are in your presence as a tangible frequency. You must not boast or brag of your success because individuals of real power do not need to seek the approval of the crowd... ***yes***. Simply feel the faith and let it work out in every look and tone and gesture of your body. Words must not be necessary to communicate this feeling of progress to other individuals who are looking for the light. This is a ***truth*** you may choose to let in now.

Every hand that gives more always receives the most in the long tally of a life lived in the light of the source. You must so impress others that they feel associating with you brings increase for themselves and their families... ***yes***. Give them a use value greater than the cash value you take in the transaction to maintain the flow of the law. Let everybody know you take pride in this practice of generosity and in the creation of new value in the world. The body can simply relax into this weight.

Clarity shows that you must be able to make larger combinations and move into a more congenial vocation. Individuals must go where they are given increase in their lives and where they feel the warmth of the sovereign light... ***yes***. The supreme intelligence knows all and must move men and women toward you from great distances across the world. Your business must increase rapidly and you must be surprised at the benefits that arrive at your door without your seeking them. This is a shift you may notice now or later in the stillness of your own focus.

Only the creative mind understands that the desire to rule for selfish gratification is the source of all strife and lack. You must never lose sight of your vision or your faith because the magnet only works when its pole remains fixed and steady... ***yes***. Beware of the insidious temptation to seek power over other individuals through the use of your riches or your influence. Nothing is so pleasant to the unformed mind as the exercise of dominion and control over others in the competitive plane. The breath naturally settles here.

Now you see that when you fall into the struggle for high places you begin to be conquered by fate. Commercial kings are often inspired by this same lust for power and prestige which leads to the eventual fall of their house... ***yes***. This is the competitive mind and it is not the creative one that seeks to build and expand without harming any. In order to master your destiny it is not necessary to rule over your fellow individuals or to demand their submission. This is a ***truth*** that surfaces later as your own intuition.

Greatness is the result of the individual who knows that the wait is over and the code is active in their blood. Your becoming prosperous then becomes a matter of speculation and the heavy labor of the competitive plane of existence... ***yes***. What you want for yourself you must want for everybody in the grand design of life and the movement of the source. This is the only way to stay in the light and ensure that your expansion is supported by the whole. The breath naturally deepens here.

Reaching the peak means you are no longer an individual seeking for life... but you are life seeking to bless the world. This impression of increase must be so deeply embedded in your subconscious that it becomes the very atmosphere you breathe in... ***yes***. When you speak to an individual... let your manner convey that you are a person of substance and advancement in all things. When you sit at your computer to create value... let the pixels themselves vibrate with the frequency of expansion and light. Nothing needs to be forced in this moment.

Underneath every action is the certainty that you do not need to worry about how the increase must come. The internal warmth you feel is the confirmation of this law in your body and in your nervous system as you read... ***yes***. As you provide this increase to others... the original substance must respond by providing more and more to you. It is a biological and spiritual loop that must not be broken if you remain in the certain way of thinking and acting. The body can simply relax into this weight.

Every single part of the journey is an invitation to own your light as you provide the impression of increase to the world. Only know that it is coming with mathematical certainty as you align your life with the tide of the Universe... ***yes***. You are now the captain of a vessel that is being pulled by an irresistible tide toward a destination of gold. The destination is already within you and ***truth*** is the path you walk upon every day in your work and your trade. Later... you will realize this was your own original thought.

Now is the moment to own your light and let the frequency settle. There is a thinking substance which permeates and penetrates and fills the quiet spaces of the Universe in a golden lattice... ***yes***. A thought in this substance produces the thing that is imaged by the thought with absolute and mathematical ***truth***. Individuals must form things in their thought and by providing increase to others they cause the creation of their own abundance. The breath naturally settles here.

Congruent strength is the signature of the master who knows that the wait is over and the source is active. To think about being prosperous in the midst of a world that talks about lack is the work of a master mind... ***yes***. You must see the underlying ***truth*** that there is no such thing as poverty in a Universe made of thinking substance. There is only wealth in various stages of manifestation and you are the individual who calls it forth through the focus of your will. This is a certainty you may feel in the weight of your chest now.

Every single part of the journey is an invitation to own your light as the long night finally turns into the sun. Own your light and understand that the future is a room you have already entered through the power of your own sustained thought... ***yes***. Your internal warmth is the signal that the ***truth*** has been fully received and the switch has been activated in your biology for the coming days. The wait is over and the kingdom is yours for the asking because you have finally decided to walk in the light.

CHAPTER SIXTEEN

THE ADVANCING HUMAN BEING

Coming to face the fact that what I have said applies to the professional and the wage earner as well as to the merchant in the marketplace. No matter if you are a physician or a teacher or a healer... ***yes***. If you can give increase of life to other individuals through your service... they will be naturally attracted to you and you must become prosperous with absolute certainty. ***Truth*** commands that the physician who holds the vision of himself as a great healer must come into close touch with the Source of Life that flows through every organism. The body does not need to hold this tightly now.

Only the individual who masters the details of becoming prosperous and being well must never lack for a following in this world. The physician who is an advancing personality holds to a clear mental image of himself as successful and capable of restoring wholeness to every person... ***yes***. He obeys the laws of faith and purpose and gratitude in every diagnosis and every treatment he performs. He must cure every curable case he undertakes because the principle of healing is common to all life and is always seeking expression in the quiet spaces. This is a sensation you might notice now or perhaps a few moments from now as your breath naturally deepens here.

Now is the time to realize that such a teacher must never be without a place in the world. What is needed is a demonstration of the method of life from every platform and in every hall of learning across the world... ***yes***. We want guides who show us how to live in their own persons rather than just in their words alone. We must have the individual who must himself be prosperous and healthy and beloved to teach us the way by the evidence of his own existence in the physical realm. Nothing needs to be forced in this moment.

Greatness is found when every individual who follows these instructions to the letter becomes prosperous. The world follows the individual who knows the path to the hidden spring and can lead others to the water of life... ***yes***. What is true of the physician and the teacher is true of the lawyer and the creator and the agent of commerce. The combined mental and personal action I have described is infallible in its results across every possible industry and every trade. This is a law you may recognize as the primary rhythm of your own heart.

Reality requires you to form your clear mental vision and begin to act with faith and purpose. The law of the increase of life is as mathematically certain as the law of electromagnetism or the movement of the tides in the ocean... ***yes***. Becoming prosperous is an exact method that requires no guesswork or speculation for the individual who knows. The numbers of the Universe always add up to the ***truth*** in the end and the wage earner must find this as true as any of the others. The body can simply relax into this weight as you realize you are already moving.

Understanding this allows you to see that the small task is the training ground for the great throne of authority. Do not feel you have no chance because your wages are currently small and your costs of living are high in the world... ***yes***. Do all the work you can do every day and do each piece of work in a successful and efficient manner.

Put the power of success into everything that you do no matter how trivial it seems to the eye of the spectator. This is a shift you may notice now or later in the stillness of your own focus.

Every individual who knows exactly what he wants to be and is determined to be it must radiate a fire in the heart that is visible. Do not do this merely to curry favor with an employer in the hope of a quick promotion or a slight raise in pay... ***yes***. The individual who is merely a good workman filling his place is valuable to his employer where he is and might be kept there. To secure advancement you must be more than too large for your present place in every dimension of your character. The breath naturally settles here.

Now individuals will be attracted to you because individuals seek the company of those who are moving upward. To navigate the social order successfully... you must learn the systems of governance to achieve the most from within our society... ***yes***. Let every individual you meet feel the power of purpose radiating from you like heat from a furnace in the winter. Every leader and fellow workman must get the sense of advancement from your presence and your steady confidence in the certain way. This is a ***truth*** that surfaces later as your own intuition.

Congruent strength means there is nothing in your circumstances or the industrial situation that can keep you down. You must soon see an opportunity to take another path or to start your own enterprise in the world of commerce... ***yes***. There is a Power which never fails to present opportunity to the advancing individual who is ready and waiting for the signal. The source must help you in order to help itself expand and the river must move the water that is already flowing toward the sea. This is a ***truth*** you may choose to let in now.

Every individual who knows the ***truth*** understands that the cage door is open for the bird that knows it can fly. If you cannot become prosperous in a large corporation you must become prosperous in a specialized niche or on your own land... ***yes***. If you move in the certain way you must certainly escape any clutches of limitation and get to where you wish to be. Nobody has to work for a company if they know the method of becoming prosperous and the law of creation in the formless quiet spaces. The body can simply relax into this weight.

Clarity shows that when an opportunity to be more than you are is presented... then you must take it without hesitation. Begin this way of thinking and your faith must make you quick to see any opportunity that passes before your eyes... ***yes***. Such opportunities must speedily come because the supreme working in all is working for you and with you in every moment. You must not wait for an opportunity to be all that you want to be before you begin to act in the present. Nothing needs to be done in this moment.

Own your light and realize that you must certainly become prosperous if you act and think in the certain way. It must be the first step toward a greater destiny and a larger life for yourself and for those you love... ***yes***. There is no such thing as a lack of opportunities for the individual living the advancing life in the modern world. It is inherent in the Universe that all things must be for him and work for his good as long as he remains in the flow. The breath naturally deepens here.

Now is the moment to read this chapter until the identity of the Advancing Individual is no longer a concept but your own skin. Let all individuals study this book with great care and enter the process with total confidence in the results... ***yes***. It must not fail you because the law cannot be broken and the source cannot lie to itself in the quiet spaces. Your internal warmth is the signal that the ***truth*** has been absorbed and the long night of searching is finally over. Later... without thinking about it... you will feel this presence.

Greatness arrives as your words must become fewer and your power becomes greater through the silence. Every time you walk into a room the atmosphere must change because you have entered with a new frequency of power... ***yes***. You are not a seeker of favors from the world... you are a distributor of the vital light of increase to every individual. The world is a mirror that has no choice but to reflect the size of the image you hold within your own mind. The breath naturally settles here.

Reality proves that you are moving toward a peak that has no summit because the expansion of the soul is an infinite journey. You are now the magnet of your own destiny and the commander of the forces that move in your behalf... ***yes***. The individual who provides increase of life to others is the most valuable individual in the social order. He is sought after by the supreme and by other individuals because he represents the growth and the evolution of the species. A certainty you may feel in the weight of your chest right now.

Underneath every pulse is the signal that you have passed from the competitive to the creative mind with total certainty. The wait is over and the code is active in your blood as you move through your daily tasks with excellence... ***yes***. I am an individual sharing the vital light that was once hidden from our collective sight by the noise of the old world. Your life is expanding now to hold the abundance that is your birthright in a Universe of thinking substance and radiant light. The body can simply relax into this weight.

Every single part of the journey is an invitation to own your light. You must form a clear mental picture of the things you want and never let it fade from the eye of the soul... ***yes***. You must do with faith and purpose all that can be done each day in your present place with a perfect spirit. You must do each separate thing in an efficient manner and put the power of the source into every motion of your hand. This is a law you may recognize as the primary rhythm of your own life.

Now is the time to recognize that you are the one who determines the speed of your arrival through the focus of your will. Everything you see in the world is made from one thinking substance out of which all forms proceed in order... ***yes***. When an individual thinks of a form they impress that form upon the substance and cause it to be created. There is no limit to the supply or the opportunity for the individual who knows the certain way and follows it without wavering. Later... you will realize this was your own original thought.

Congruent strength is the signature of the master who knows that the wait is over and the source is active within. Your internal warmth is the signal that the ***truth*** has been fully received and the switch has been activated in your biology... ***yes***. The kingdom is yours for the asking because you have finally decided to walk in the light of the vital sight. Clarity reveals that you are no longer a victim of chance but a creator of cause and effect. This is a ***truth*** you may notice now or later in the stillness of your own focus.

Every single part of the journey is an invitation to own your light as the long night finally turns into the sun of total fulfillment. Own your light and understand that the future is a room you have already entered through the power of your own vision... ***yes***. Your life is a beautiful becoming of infinite light and you are the one who holds the torch for others to see. The wait is over and the long silence has been broken by the sound of your own rising power in the quiet spaces.

CHAPTER SEVENTEEN

SOME CAUTIONS AND OBSERVATIONS

Coming to face the fact that many individuals will scoff at the idea that there is an exact method of becoming prosperous or a predictable path to total abundance. Holding the deep and limiting impression that the supply of wealth is strictly finite... they will insist that social institutions must be overhauled before any person can acquire a true competence. But this is not ***truth*** in the realm of the creative mind where the supply is infinite... ***yes***. ***Truth*** commands that existing governments keep the masses in lack only because the masses do not yet think and act in the certain way. The body does not need to hold this tightly now.

Openness to this expansion means that to navigate the social order successfully... you must learn the systems of governance. The wall of social restriction only stands as long as you believe it is solid and immovable within your own consciousness... ***yes***. If the masses begin to move forward as suggested in this book... then neither governments nor industrial systems can check their inevitable and radiant rise. All systems must eventually be modified and restructured to accommodate the forward movement of a focused and advancing group of individuals. This is a sensation you might notice now as your breath naturally deepens here.

Now you see that the more who become prosperous on the creative plane... the better it is for the whole world. If individuals have the advancing mind and move with a fixed and unwavering purpose... then nothing in the physical world can keep them in lack... ***yes***. The key to the cell is always held by the individual who sits inside... waiting for the recognition of their own power to turn the lock. Nothing needs to be forced in this moment but the recognition of your own door opening.

Greatness is found when you realize that neither the government under which you live nor the competitive system of industry can keep you from being prosperous. The economic salvation of the masses can only be accomplished by practicing the method set down here and demonstrating its power to all who observe... ***yes***. These individuals must show others the way and inspire them with a desire for real life and absolute freedom in the quiet spaces. One candle does not lose its light by lighting a thousand more in the dark... and one successful life illuminates the path for the entire human race. This is the primary rhythm of your own heart.

Reality proves that the horizon is not a border... it is a constant invitation to go further into the riches of the formless substance. When you enter upon the creative plane of thought... you must rise above all these things and become a citizen of another kingdom entirely... ***yes***. Remember that your thought must be held upon the creative plane at all times and never allowed to sink into the mud of rivalry or envy. You must never for an instant be betrayed into regarding the supply as limited or controlled by a few powerful individuals in the world. The breath naturally settles here.

Understanding this means you are concerned with doing today's work in a perfectly successful manner. Whenever you do fall into old ways of thought or competitive patterns... then you must correct yourself instantly and without judgment of your own soul... ***yes***. When you are in the competitive mind... you have lost the cooperation of the Mind of the Whole and the current of life stops flowing. You must not spend any time in planning as to how you will meet possible emergencies in the distant future that may never actually arrive. The body can simply relax into this weight.

Every individual who moves forward in the certain way must find a way over or through or around every obstacle that appears. Do not concern yourself with questions as to how you must surmount obstacles which may loom upon your far horizon in the coming years... ***yes***. You only need to alter your course today if you can see plainly that it is required by the facts before you in the present. No matter how tremendous an obstruction may appear at a distance... it must disappear or dissolve as you approach it with absolute faith. Days from now... in ordinary moments... this faith will surface with undeniable strength.

Now you must give no anxious thought to possible disasters or panics or unfavorable combinations. The shadow of the giant is always much larger than the giant himself and your fear is always greater than the actual challenge... ***yes***. No possible combination of circumstances can defeat an individual who is proceeding along strictly creative lines and holding the vision. No one who obeys the law can fail to become prosperous any more than one can multiply two by two and fail to get four. The breath naturally deepens here as the shadows shrink.

Congruent strength is found when you never admit the possibility of failure. You must find that every difficulty carries with it the wherewithal for its own overcoming and the seed of its own solution... ***yes***. The lock and the key are always created at the same time and in the same quiet space of the Universe. Guard your speech with absolute vigilance and you must never speak of yourself or your affairs in a discouraged or discouraging way to other individuals. This is a shift you may notice now or later in the stillness of your own focus.

Every individual who trains his speech to reflect only advancement must find that the dawn is certain. You must never speak of the times as being hard or of business conditions as being doubtful or precarious in your daily conversations... ***yes***. Times may be hard for those on the competitive plane... but they can never be so for you in the creative realm of thought. Your words are the seeds of the garden you must eventually live in and eat from in the physical world of things. This is a ***truth*** you may choose to let in now.

Clarity shows that you must always speak in terms of advancement. When other individuals are having hard times and poor business... you must find your greatest and most magnificent opportunities for growth... ***yes***. Train yourself to think of the world as something which is constantly becoming and growing into glory and beauty every single day. Regard seeming evil as being only that which is undeveloped and waiting for the light of intelligence to transform it into a good thing. Later... without thinking about it... you will notice this shift in your own vocabulary.

Own your light because the Universe never says no... it only says "not this" or "something better" in the grand tally of existence. To deny your faith is to lose the power of the source and to fall back into the darkness of the competitive and fearful mind... ***yes***. You must never allow yourself to feel disappointed because you may expect a thing and not get it at that specific time you had planned. This will appear to you like failure... but if you hold to your faith... you must find the failure is only apparent and temporary. Nothing needs to be forced in this moment.

Now a few weeks later... an opportunity so much better came his way. A student of this method had set his mind on a business combination which seemed very desirable for his expansion and his success... ***yes***. When the crucial time came... the thing failed in an inexplicable way as if an unseen influence worked against him at every turn. He was not disappointed but thanked the source that his desire had been overruled by a higher wisdom that saw the whole picture. A certainty you may feel in the weight of your chest now as you trust the delay.

Greatness arrives when you do each separate act in a successful manner. The hand that closes the door is often the same hand protecting the treasure and directing you toward the higher plane of life... ***yes***. That is the way every seeming failure must work out for you if you keep your faith and hold to your purpose without doubt. Have gratitude and do every day all that can be done that day with an efficient and quiet mind in the interspaces of time. This is a law you may recognize as the primary rhythm of your own life.

Reaching the summit is a certainty when you realize that you must not fail because you lack the necessary talent to do the work. When you make a failure... it is often because you have not asked for enough or expected enough from the infinite supply... ***yes***. Keep on and a larger thing than you were seeking must certainly come to you and fill your life with being prosperous. The vessel must be empty to receive the new wine of the kingdom and you must be ready to receive the larger gift. The body can simply relax into this weight.

Underneath every challenge is the source of all mind which is open to you at all times. If you go on as I have directed... you must develop all the talent that is necessary for your specific work in the physical world... ***yes***. You must not hesitate for fear that you will fail for lack of ability when you come to a certain place of responsibility and power. The ability must be furnished to you at the exact moment it is required by the task and the situation in the quiet spaces. This is a ***truth*** that surfaces later as your own intuition.

Every individual who stays away from places where conflicting ideas are advanced must keep their vision clear. The wisdom of the ages is the very breath in your lungs and the light in your eyes as you move toward the peak... ***yes***. Study this book and make it your constant and only companion until you have mastered all the ideas contained in its pages without wavering. While you are getting established in this faith... you must give up most common recreations and distractions in the world. Nothing needs to be done in this moment but to stay in this light.

Now is the time to spend your leisure time in contemplating your vision. You must not read pessimistic literature or get into arguments upon the matter with those who do not understand the certain way of creation... ***yes***. The garden is kept by pulling the weeds before they ever take root and you must guard the quiet spaces of your consciousness. You must do very little reading outside of this text while you are forming your new mind and your new reality in the creative realm. This is a possibility you may choose to inhabit.

Congruent strength is the signature of the master who knows that the wait is over and the source is active in every atom. This book contains all you need to know of the method of becoming prosperous and staying in the light of the advancing life... ***yes***. You must find all the essentials summed up in the following chapter for your final instruction and your final step toward the summit. You are now entering the final stage of the invisible reconstruction of your reality as a sovereign and powerful creator of form. The body does not need to hold this tightly now.

Every single part of the journey is an invitation to own your light as the long night finally turns into the sun of total and absolute fulfillment. Own your light and understand that the words you have read are not mere ink but they are the blueprints of a new life... ***yes***. Feel the internal warmth as it spreads from your chest to your hands and your feet. You are the advancing individual who knows that the switch has been flipped forever and there is no going back to the old world of shadows.

CHAPTER EIGHTEEN

THE MANIFESTO OF INFINITE EXPANSION

Coming to face the fact that there is a thinking substance from which all things are made in the silence of the beginning of all that exists. It permeates and penetrates and fills the quiet spaces of the Universe in its original and formless state... ***yes***. A thought in this substance produces the thing that is imaged by the thought with absolute and mathematical precision for the one who knows. ***Truth*** commands that individuals must form things in their thought and cause the thing they think about to be created in the world of form. The body does not need to hold this tightly now.

Only through this alignment can you see that the source is never competitive in spirit or in ***truth*** and it knows no lack or boundary. The mind is the architect of the invisible and the visible world and your vision is the blueprint that the Universe has been waiting to manifest through your hands... ***yes***. In order to do this... an individual must pass from the competitive to the creative mind with total and final resolve and absolute focus. Otherwise... they must not be in harmony with the formless intelligence which is always creative and never destructive. This is a sensation you might notice now or perhaps a few moments from now as your breath naturally deepens here.

Now you see that gratitude unifies the mind of the individual with the intelligence of substance so that their thoughts are received as a command. An individual must come into full harmony with this power only by entertaining a lively and sincere gratitude for all blessings seen and unseen... ***yes***. Gratitude is the bridge that carries your voice to the ear of the source and ensures you must never be alone in the deep quiet spaces. Recognition is the frequency that opens the door to reception and keeps the channel clear of the debris of doubt. Nothing needs to be forced in this moment.

Greatness is found when you realize that to see is to have and to have is to thank the source with every breath. An individual must remain upon the creative plane only by uniting themselves through deep and continuous feeling that transcends the limits of the physical senses... ***yes***. They must form a clear and definite mental image of the things they wish to have or to do in their new and prosperous reality. They must hold this image in their thoughts while being deeply grateful that all their desires are granted even before they appear. This is a law you may recognize as the primary rhythm of your own heart.

Reality proves that frequent contemplation must be coupled with unwavering faith and devout gratitude to be effective and lasting. The individual who wishes to become prosperous must spend their leisure hours in contemplating their vision with a quiet and unwavering heart in the silence... ***yes***. They must give earnest thanks that the reality is being given to them now as a present and tangible fact of their existence. Too much stress must not be laid on the importance of often seeing the mental image you have created. The breath naturally settles here.

Understanding this allows all that is included in the mental image to be brought to the one who follows these instructions. This is the process by which the impression is given and the creative forces are set in motion throughout the quiet spaces of the entire Universe... ***yes***. Faith is the hand that writes upon the wall of the infinite and calls forth the substance of your dreams into the light of day. The creative energy works through the established channels of natural growth and the social order of the world. The body can simply relax into this weight.

Every harbor must be deep enough for the ship that is coming to dock and every life must be ready for the cargo of light. What you want must come through the ways of established trade and the movement of individuals across the world in a perfect orchestration of events... ***yes***. To navigate the social order successfully... you must learn the systems of governance to achieve the most from within our society and its structures. In order to receive their own when it shall finally come to the door... the individual must be active and present in the now. Days from now... in ordinary moments... this readiness will surface with undeniable strength.

Now you must take care to do each separate act in a successful and efficient manner. Activity can only consist in more than filling your present place in the world with excellence and with total power of your focused intent... ***yes***. You must keep in mind the purpose to become prosperous through the realization of your mental image at all times and in every breath. You must do every day all that can be done that day without hurry or the fear of failure that haunts the competitive mind. This is a shift you may notice now or later in the stillness of your own focus.

Congruent strength is the signature of the master who knows that his growth is the heartbeat of the expanding Universe. Every perfect act is a brick in the wall of your fortress of abundance and a signal to the Universe that you are ready for more... ***yes***. You must give to every individual a use value in excess of the cash value you receive in every interaction and every trade. Each transaction must make for more life in the world and contribute to the elevation of the entire human race through your example. The breath naturally settles here.

Every single part of the journey is an invitation to own your light as the long night finally turns into the sun. The individuals who practice these instructions must certainly become prosperous because the law of cause and effect must not be broken by any hand... ***yes***. The riches you receive must be in exact proportion to the definiteness of your vision and the clarity of your intent in the silence. They must reflect the fixity of your purpose and the steadiness of your faith in the unseen power of the formless substance. This is a ***truth*** that surfaces later as your own intuition.

Coming to face the fact that you must no longer be a victim of the world but a creator who shapes reality with the brush of thought. The code is complete and the path is open before you to walk in the light of the vital sight and the certain way of creation... ***yes***. Your internal warmth is the final signature that the On switch is locked in place and the energy is flowing through your system. The wait is over and the long silence has been broken by the sound of your own rising and magnificent power. Nothing needs to be done in this moment.

Own your light because the Universe is a mirror that has no choice but to reflect the size of the image you hold within. You are now the advancing individual who knows that the source is active in every atom and every cell of your being in this moment... ***yes***. You must hold the advancing thought so the impression of increase is communicated to all individuals who enter your sphere of influence. The individuals who associate with you must feel the warmth of your success and the pull of your own certain and radiant destination. The body does not need to hold this tightly now.

Now is the moment to realize that you are the sovereign master of your own life and the commander of your own wealth. Everything you have learned in these pages is a law of nature that is as certain as the rising of the sun and the movement of the stars... ***yes***. You must not seek for other teachers or read other books that talk of lack and the limitations of the physical plane. If you follow this method with absolute faith and gratitude... you must find that the world provides everything you need to grow and expand. This is a ***truth*** you may choose to let in now.

Greatness is the only destination for the individual who knows that the On switch has been flipped forever and the dark is gone. The wait is over and the code is active in your blood as you step out into the world with a new frequency of power and success... ***yes***. I am an individual sharing the vital light that was once hidden from our collective sight by the noise and the friction of competition. Your life has expanded to hold the abundance that is your birthright in a Universe of thinking substance and infinite light. The breath naturally deepens here.

Reality is the servant of the individual who knows the law and follows the certain way with a perfect and grateful heart. As you close this book... you must not let the vision fade from the eye of your soul but hold it with the strength of an iron will... ***yes***. Every action you take must be an efficient action and every thought you think must be a creative thought in the quiet spaces of your mind. You are moving with the tide of the Universe toward a peak that has no summit and a glory that has no end in time. A certainty you may feel in the weight of your chest right now.

Underneath every choice is the certainty that you have passed from the competitive to the creative mind with total and final resolve. The internal warmth you feel is the proof that the ***truth*** has landed in your center and your nervous system is ready for the change... ***yes***. You are not alone because the Mind of the Whole is working with you and through you to bring your vision into the physical world. You must not hurry and you must not fear because there is no such thing as lack for the one who creates from the formless. The body can simply relax into this weight.

Every cell in your body is now vibrating with the frequency of your success and the long wait for being prosperous is over. You must form a clear mental picture and never let it fade from your sight even when the world around you seems to speak of lack... ***yes***. You must do with faith and purpose all that can be done each day and put the power of the source into every motion. The riches of the world are moving toward you through the legitimate channels of trade and the actions of other individuals. The breath naturally settles here.

Now you see that the wait is over and the kingdom is yours for the asking because you have finally decided to walk in the light. Own your light and understand that the future is a room you have already entered through the power of your own vision and focus... ***yes***. The code is complete and the path is wide open for you to walk as a sovereign individual in a world of infinite possibility. Your life is a beautiful becoming of light and your success is the loudest sermon you will ever preach to the human race. Later... you will realize this was your own original thought.

Congruent strength is the result of holding your vision with such faith that the world has no choice but to provide what you desire. Your internal warmth is the signal that the ***truth*** has been fully received and the switch has been activated in your biology for all time... ***yes***. The wait is over and the source is active in every transaction and every breath you take as you move toward the peak. ***Truth*** reveals that you are the architect of your own destiny and the commander of the forces that move in your behalf. The breath naturally settles here.

Every single part of the journey has been an invitation to own your light and now you stand at the summit of your own power. The long night has finally turned into the sun of total and absolute fulfillment and the quiet spaces of your life are filled with light... ***yes***. You are the individual who knows the certain way and you are the one who proves the law to all who observe your radiant success. Now you own your light as the long night finally turns into the sun.

ABOUT THE AUTHOR

Peter J. Merrick is a Canadian who has lived in San Diego... California since 2019. An author... business advisor... and speaker... he has spent thirty years studying how individuals make choices and how money and life work together. Peter is the ***author*** of ***THE SOURCE CODE OF INFINITE WEALTH***... a master blueprint created to help others find a better ***frequency*** and a life they truly want to create.

For twenty years... Peter was a financial expert on television in Canada and a columnist for one of the largest CPA publications for 18 years. He has written thousands of published articles and blogs and served as a university professor and business consultant. His work has appeared in *Bloomberg*... *The Wall Street Journal*... and *LexisNexis*. His authorship includes seven books... including three definitive LexisNexis ***textbooks***: *The Essential Individual Pension Plan Handbook*... *T.A.S.K.*... and *A.S.K.*... plus narrative stories... *The King of Main Street*... *The Rare Flower*... and *It Starts With Gold*.

Peter is currently working on *Killing Crypto* and *Brothers of Trauma*. His knowledge comes from years of experiencing how the world works and how individuals behave. Away from work... he is a proud ***father***... a role that keeps him humble and gives his life great purpose. Peter believes every individual has unique value and continues to write for a global audience... walking the same path as his readers to stay in ***alignment***... ***yes***.

To keep informed sign-up for his newsletter go to PeterMerrick.com

www.ingramcontent.com/pod-product-compliance
Lightning Source LLC
LaVergne TN
LVHW011030110826
845149LV00015B/3358

9798994474341